the Good Stuff

A GUIDEBOOK TO FINISHING STRONG

 HAVILAH CUNNINGTON

Havilah Cunnington

I always knew God had a plan for others' lives, but never felt God could use me. I struggled with learning disabilities throughout my school years, which caused me to have great insecurity about my value and worth. It wasn't until the age of 17, as I was sitting in a car with friends on my way to a party, when I heard the voice of God speak to my heart, "There is more to life than this! I have called you. Come follow me." I spoke out in that moment, telling those in the car that I had a call on my life and they were welcome to come with me, but I was going to serve God.

I remember walking into our house when I got home, kneeling by my bed and saying these simple words, "God, I'm not much. I'm young, I'm a girl with no special gifting. But if You can use anyone, You can use me." Now, thinking back to that day, it makes me laugh how I'd hoped the heavens would have opened up, with angels descending and ascending on a heavenly ladder – that didn't happen and I didn't need it to. God heard my cry and He was at work to accomplish His perfect will in my life.

By 19, my twin sister Deborah and I were traveling all over California preaching, teaching and singing at any place that would have us. By 21, we had been in seven different states and Mexico teaching about Jesus and His great plan for this generation!

Now almost two decades later I still believe today is the Church's finest hour, if we choose to live with passion, purpose and walk in power. I'm passionate about seeing individuals encounter God in a real way and seek to blow the lid off common misconceptions, personal limitations and powerless living. My heart and passion is to inspire and challenge others to become all God has designed them to be.

Today I wear many hats: wife, mom, pastor, teacher, daughter and friend. My husband Ben and I were leaders at The Rock of Roseville Church for the past 15 years, but have recently made a huge transition by moving to Redding, California, to be the Directors of Moral Revolution. We enjoy spending time with our four young sons: Judah, Hudson, Grayson and Beckham.

PREFACE
The Good Stuff

It was my favorite time again! We were having people over and my mom was busy preparing the house for a day full of festivities. Vacuuming rooms, dusting, wiping windows, and preparing food was just the beginning of all the work that went into this seemingly flawless gathering later on in the day. As we set the table, we heard mom's voice ring out down the hall, "Don't forget to use the good stuff!" We all knew what she meant. My Italian grandmother, immigrant turned congressman's wife, with impeccable taste had generously shuffled out her elaborate collection of fine china between her five children. My dad's set of dishes were definitely going to be used today. We gently and cautiously pulled them out, with their gold trim graciously holding the edges of the bone white centers. They were exquisite!

There was something my family understood about the words the "good stuff." We all knew what it meant. It was the best we had. It was the stuff we saved. It was our best revealed.

I think Jesus knew a little bit about the good stuff. He loves to save the best for last. At a wedding where He performed His first miracle, the words may have run out over the crowd, "Wait! Is this the good stuff? You saved the best for last!"

It's that special perfume you leave on your dresser just for date night. The bottle of wine tucked deep in the cellar waiting for just the right occasion. The glamorous dress hanging in the back of the closet waiting, just waiting, for the proposal. It's the prime piece of meat tucked way back in the freezer. The classic car parked in the garage only driven to the special event you've been waiting for all year. The good stuff.

We do it all the time! The best stuff. The finest stuff. Unsurpassed. The Good Stuff study is all about getting all the best stuff in one place. It's about taking all the good stuff hidden in the Word and bringing it out into the open so you can live the life God intended you to live. The stuff you simply must know to help nurture your soul and feed your spirit. It's the prime meat of the word that truly satisfies you, and gets you from point A to point B in a matter of moments. It's your best garments that you can wrap yourself in, feeling covered and confident. It's the stuff that just works! Not because these are good ideas or practical advice but because it's the Word of God.

And you know something? When you taste the good stuff, you just know it. Just like the wedding guests and the groom at the Jewish wedding. They couldn't help themselves. They joyfully uttered, "This is the GOOD STUFF!" It's impossible to miss. The Word of God, when used correctly and applied humbly, will taste sweeter than the sweetest thing you've ever tasted. It will leave you fuller than you've ever felt. The richness and quality will find no equal in your life. So, let's feast on the goodness of God and the Word He has given us. He has truly brought us to a banqueting table and His banner over us is love!

Havilah

WEEK ONE

ENGAGE YOUR WILL

We begin our entire study looking at one of the most powerful and highly underestimated areas of our spiritual life — the human will. In the Garden of Eden, when God first created Adam and Eve, He gave them a free will. He did this so that they would be free; free to choose their own way in life and free to choose relationship. They were to be responsible for their own actions. God didn't do this to be separate from them, but to be close to them. How does that work? Because love demanded or controlled isn't real love; only love freely chosen and freely given is authentic.

Understanding your will is very important. Your will is where all your determinations and decisions come from. It is very powerful and without bringing it under the submission of your spirit, it will be subject to being influenced by your enemy or controlled by your emotions. The human will is so powerful it can override any decision, desire, commitment or loyalty.

Jesus revealed a defining truth about our human will in the garden when He said, *"Not my will but yours be done."* Jesus had his own human will, apart from the Father's. So do we. We learn very quickly that God does not veto our will to accomplish His. We also learn that it's not easy to see His will come to pass while ours is at work.

So, what does a Christ follower's life and will look like? Does our will get renewed? Does it ever finally look like God's will? I would suggest it does get renewed, but only by being laid down and surrendered. That's the place where we still feel the pull, desire and even motive, but out of love we utter the same words as our Savior, "Not my will but yours." It's in the moment of yielded strength that we build character. We build trust. We build humility.

And finally we learn that our will is something God gave to us from the beginning of time to help us. Your will, when yielded and used in the way it was designed, can catapult you into the will of God faster than anything else. It's the place of determination and sheer willpower that will have you holding out for the promises of God. Never giving up and getting what others so easily walked away from. Your will was designed to give you staying power. So all your resolution and strength would be focused on what God wants to do in and through you.

DAY 1
Lead and Follow

For as many as are led by the Spirit of God, they are the sons of God.
— *Romans 8:14*

Finney was the name of our family dog growing up. I remember him always wanting to go for walks. He loved them! Finney would jump around with excitement, running to the door, barking as if to say, "I thought you would never ask!" We'd put on his leash and off we'd go. It was the highlight of his day! But as a puppy, Finney was horrible on our family walks. He would run ahead only to be choked by his leash down the street. He would run to the side and, of course, get caught on a branch, while we yelled at him to back up and move. When he was finally done with all the running around, he would slow right down so we would have to drag him along, eventually carrying him. As Finney grew, he began to understand how it all worked and eventually it was rare that we would have to drag him or slow him down. He would allow himself to be led smoothly, humbly and maturely.

In chapter 8 of Romans Paul writes these words in verse 14: *"For as many as are led by the Spirit of God, they are the sons of God."* In the Greek, the verb is reversed so it reads, *"For as many as by the Spirit are being led, they are the sons of God."* This version puts the Holy Spirit at the front of the verse, and we are placed behind Him. The story about Finney illustrates perfectly what this verse in the Bible is saying. The Greek word for "led" is the word *ago*, which simply means 'to lead'. It was often used to portray an animal that was being led by a rope tied around its neck. Once tied to the rope, the animal willingly followed wherever their owner led them.[1]

---

1 Renner, Rick. *Sparkling Gems (Page 19)* Published 2003. Print.

I've found in my spiritual life that my willingness to be led is the key to living well. If we allow the Holy Spirit to lead us we are promised fruitful lives. The key to being willing to be led is trust. It's not necessarily easy to trust that it is the right way especially when it feels unnatural for us, however we must believe that God is leading us into life even if we don't want to go that way. As we submit to the process, He is faithful to us! Remember, Jesus called the Holy Spirit the *"Spirit of Truth"* (John 16:13) to help us understand that He can be trusted. We are promised to reap a good harvest if we sow good seeds. We cannot see the future, but He can. We do not always know what to do, but He does. He has the heavenly perspective of seeing us from beginning to end. Knowing that He sees it all helps us trust and allows us to lean back into the arms of our Father to be led.

It's important to point out that the root word for "led" (ago) is also the root word for the word agon, which is where we get the word agony. Like the word means today, it describes an intense conflict, such as the struggle in a wrestling match or, when it comes to this area of trust, the struggle of our human will with our spirit. This gives us a clear picture of what's really going on inside of us. We don't naturally want to be led; we want to go our own way, left to do as we please, satisfying our fleshly desires and living to please ourselves. If we allow this fleshly desire to rule, we will reap the reward which Galatians 6:8 calls corruption: *"For he who sows to the flesh will of the flesh reap corruption, but he who sows to the spirit will of the spirit reap everlasting life."*

Jesus called us sheep. If you've ever studied sheep you know that's not a compliment. Sheep need to be led. Sheep have no way of protecting themselves, so they need an able shepherd to keep them unified and safe. When a certain sheep has a tendency to run off, do you know what the shepherd does? He breaks its legs. He then gently places it on his shoulders. He hand feeds it, carrying it until the leg is mended. This is what our Good Shepherd does with us! He allows the world to break us down until we can't help but be dependent on Him.

When the Holy Spirit comes to lead us, we tend to feel a struggle. We don't like it! We know it's good for us but it's not easy and our flesh hates it. But we must remember what Galatians says about this: if we want to reap the reward of a fruitful life, there is no way around it — we have to deal with our flesh.

Today, I want to encourage you to submit to the tugging and leading of the Holy Spirit. Sometimes it's so gentle you might miss it if you are not tuning in to Him. He is a gentleman and He will not force you to do anything. Just because we say it with our mouths does not mean we are automatically led by Him. We have to be committed to obedience. We have to surrender ourselves one hundred percent. When we follow His lead, it's meant to be easier. When we struggle with following Him, questioning His will, life is HARD. Be careful not to demand that He tell you the whole story before you follow Him. Part of being under His Lordship means being subject to Him. Yes, it's a partnership, but it's not a plurality. He is the leader and we are the followers. He is the Shepherd and we are the sheep. He is the one guiding us and we are the ones responding.

MY PRAYER FOR TODAY
Lord, I know You know what is best for me. I really struggle at times being willing to follow You. I understand the enemy loves to lie to me, telling me I can't trust You. But today I surrender again! I want to be led. I want to hear Your voice in the stillness of the day and respond to you wholeheartedly. I confess I'm not always good at being led. I can easily be self sufficient. I ask You, Holy Spirit, to help me! Give me the

faith to trust in a God I cannot see. Give me the strength to sit back and rely on my Good Shepherd. I want to follow You exactly where You are leading.

I ask this in Jesus' name!

MY CONFESSION FOR TODAY

I have a Good Shepherd! He is taking good care of me. I confess I'm learning to follow Him in a greater way. I'm getting better at hearing His voice and when I wander, I return at the sound of His call. I'm not sitting around taking care of myself. No! I have a God who is totally and fully involved in helping me. I declare I'm choosing to walk in one hundred percent obedience. I'm not picking and choosing what I will do for Him. I'm going all the way! I'm not looking back. I confess I need Him more and more, and my strength is being renewed as I wait on Him. He can be trusted and I'm trusting! I'm walking with Him and joyfully following His leadership.

I declare this in Jesus' name!

MY ACTION STEPS FOR TODAY

1. Take a moment and read Psalm 23 aloud.
   Try to emphasize reading it in the first person.
   Insert yourself into the text!

2. Go online to www.biblegateway.com and look up the chapter in the Amplified Version. Take time to meditate on each verse and thank God for who He is to you at each stage of your journey.

DAY 2
The Fruit Of Meekness

But the fruit of the Spirit is love, joy, peace, longsuffering, gentleness, goodness, faith, meekness, temperance: against such there is no law.
—*Galatians 5:22–23*

Take a moment to open your Bible and read Galatians 5:22–23. Notice meekness is hanging out right along with the other fruit of the Spirit — love, joy, peace, longsuffering, gentleness, goodness, and faith. Wow, meekness must be some pretty POWERFUL stuff!

Meekness... really? I've always been under the impression that a person of meekness was someone who was quiet, easily blending into the crowd and, honestly, a little weak. Not until I began to study what meekness means did I come to understand it as a very potent attribute.

The word meekness in this passage comes from the word prautes. It means the attitude or demeanor of a person who is forbearing, patient, and slow to respond in anger; one who remains in control of himself in the face of insults or injuries. The picture of meekness is a strong-willed person who has learned to submit his will to a higher power.[2] Therefore, you could say that he isn't weak at all but that he's controlled. The flesh loves to rage out of control. If your flesh was allowed to have its way, it would overwork, over-worry, overeat, overindulge, and literally run itself to death. But we are called to be meek!

---

2 Renner, Rick. Sparkling Gems (Page 754) Published 2003. Print.

We are called to have a will that is completely submitted to the Spirit of God. He is the only one who knows when enough is enough! He is truly the One who has our best interests at heart; He knows and loves us more than we do ourselves. He is completely trustworthy! But in order for meekness to grow in our lives, we must surrender our strength. Not give it up but simply and powerfully lay it at the feet of Jesus. Ask Him what He thinks. Give Him access to our abilities, our strengths, and our gifts — all of it.

In the middle of the book of James it reads, *"Receive with meekness the implanted word."* Isn't that incredible! The way we received the Word, even the way that we read the Word, is important to God so that it can become inserted, buried in us, like a seed is planted in the soil. I would suggest that receiving the Word with meekness looks like someone who, upon hearing the Word, takes it deep to heart with a desire to apply it. They trust the Word. The opposite could look like someone who hears the Word and is apprehensive. They receive the Word with a skeptical eye, picking it apart and applying only what seems right to them. We need to come to our Bibles with a desire to receive and apply. A heart position that says, "Lord I'm here to receive from You! I lay down my previous knowledge and experience in order to hear a fresh word from You. I give You permission to give me divine wisdom, guidance, and counsel. I'm here to receive!"

You'll know that the Spirit is producing meekness in your life when you have self-control even in difficult circumstances. Most times, in trying situations, your emotions rage out of control; they come up from somewhere inside of us, flood our being, and take over in the moment. Part of living with the fruit of meekness is living with emotional control. Even in the midst of strong and, at times, rampant feelings, we will have an ability to surrender the emotion and live according to an orderly spirit.

Speaking of outbursts of emotion, did you know that "meekness" was also used in a medical sense to denote soothing medication to calm the angry mind? I'm reminded immediately of the scripture that says, *"A soft answer turns away wrath."* I would suggest it could be translated, "A meek answer heals an unhealthy response." It's that powerful!

MY PRAYER FOR TODAY

Lord, I ask You to renew my spirit within me today. I thank You that as a part of living in You and allowing Your Spirit to develop in me, I reap the fruit of meekness. I ask You to help me to surrender my strength today. You have not called me to be weak or passive, but rather to live with a surrendered will. Give me eyes to see what You are doing. Help me to lay down my desire to control; which comes out of fear. I don't need to fear because Your love casts it out! Help me to receive what You're saying with meekness. Don't let my ego get in the way. I want to be a child of God who listens and receives with an open spirit. I pray this in Jesus Name! Amen.

MY CONFESSION FOR TODAY

I confess I'm not weak. I'm a strong child of God and He has put His strength in me. I can carry my strength and still be a surrendered follower of Christ. Today, I'm going to surrender my strength to the power of God. Because I trust God and what He says about me, I'm going to do what He asks. I will not control. I will not fear. I will not worry. I will trust God. I will, in meekness, receive the Word. When I read it, I'm going to read it like I'm hearing it for the very first time. I'm not suspicious. I'm a believer. I'm a child of God. I have the fruit of the Spirit living in me. I have the ability to cultivate meekness in my life. I confess this in Jesus' name! Amen.

MY ACTION STEPS FOR TODAY

1. Grab your Bible and pick out a familiar verse. Set your heart to receive it differently. Ask the Lord to help you receive this passage with meekness. Did you notice a difference?

2. Take out a clean piece of paper and write out your top five gifts or strengths. They may not be something that you've perfected, but they're something that you find you have some strength in. Take a moment to meditate on the list and ask the Lord to gently remind you to use these strengths with a meek spirit.

3. Find a way to serve someone today. Whether it's a stranger, a colleague, a family member or friend. In meekness, use your gifts to serve them without any expectations or something in return and with a happy heart!

DAY 3
Travel Guide

However, when He, the Spirit of truth, has come, He will guide you into all truth; for He will not speak on His own authority, but whatever He hears He will speak; and He will tell you things to come. —John 16:13

Yielding our will and living out of a meek spirit has so many benefits. God never asked us to live out something without it having a deep and abiding benefit to our lives, both naturally and spiritually. He wants to lead us not to only prove we can be led, but He has a heart to lead us into all good things.

Jesus said in the book of John, chapter 16 that the Holy Spirit will tell you things to come. The word "tell" is a Greek word odegeo and is a word used for a guide who shows a traveler the safest course to an unknown country. This is a perfect way to describe the Holy Spirit! He is not only a comforter, but He is the guide who is trying to get us to a future point of destination in the safest way possible.[3]

Think about the possibilities for a moment; all your dreams, plans, and hopes whirling around your heart, your mind and your will. All the hours, days, even years spent wondering how you're going to get there. Should I take this course? Should I marry that person? Is it time to have kids now? Should I go for that? It's impossible to see what is still unseen, but Jesus gives us hope! He says you don't have to be afraid. You have a guide, a tour guide. A guide that will take you and lead you exactly where you need to go. Into a place of deep fulfillment, purpose and peace. He'll lead you to do what you were created to do and be who you were created to be.

---

3 Renner, Rick. Sparkling Gems (Page 646) Published 2003. Print.

The danger comes when we haven't yielded our will to God; our desire to be in charge is very strong and can take over unannounced! Many times we high-five the Holy Spirit with an, "I'll take it from here!" or "I got this!" This is where many of us get into trouble. The Bible says there is a way that seems right to a man but in the end it leads to death (Proverbs 16:25). I believe there are many times in our lives where things will seem right to us but without the leading of the Holy Spirit and His perfect guidance, we will get ourselves in trouble. We need His perfect guidance, His foresight, His protection and navigation for the journey ahead of us.

Lastly, if the Holy Spirit speaks something to you, OBEY Him! Our relationship with Him is based on trust. It's based on believing Him. What if every person in our lives that we are in relationship with consistently proves themselves trustworthy, but each time they say something we continue to be suspicious and doubtful? Chances are it's not a very secure relationship. In fact, it's going to eventually disintegrate because every good, healthy relationship has trust at its foundation. If you are trustworthy then what you say to me I believe and therefore I will let you in to my heart and life. It works the same way with the Holy Spirit. If you are suspicious and doubtful each time He speaks, don't be surprised if you lack a strong relationship with Him. It will damage your relationship with Him and His purpose for your life. He's not really driving the car if you continually grab the wheel.

MY PRAYER FOR TODAY
Lord, I thank You that you have always had a plan for my life. Even while You were on the earth, You were setting me up for success. You had it all planned out! I thank You that You sent Your Holy Spirit not only as a comfort, but as a guide. A perfect guide to show me the safest course through this journey of life. Father I thank You that He knows exactly

where You are taking me and He is ready and willing to get me there. He really loves me and is for me and can do nothing apart from show love toward me. I thank You that I can trust Him and that He does not lie to me. Help me to see what you are doing in my life and to trust You when I do not understand it all. I pray this in Jesus name! Amen.

MY CONFESSION FOR TODAY

I confess I have the perfect tour guide who will lead me in my purpose, plan and destiny. The Holy Spirit has got my back! He is the perfect navigator through all the things I need to walk through today. I confess I am not lost. I am not overwhelmed. I am not confused. The Holy Spirit is leading me through valleys and up mountains and He's doing a perfect job. I'm on my way! When the Holy Spirit speaks to me, I'm going to listen immediately. I'm not going to delay. I won't hesitate. I'm not suspicious or doubtful. I'm going to believe Him. The Holy Spirit does not lie to me. He loves me!

I confess this in Jesus' name! Amen.

MY ACTION STEPS FOR TODAY

1. If you've noticed a pattern in your life where you can't seem to let go of control, take a moment and submit your heart to Him. Many times there has been a pattern of people in our lives breaking our trust, which makes it hard for us to trust God. Break agreement with the lie that says, " I'm the only one I can trust to take care of me." Let the Holy Spirit go deep and allow Him to reveal any lies about His nature and character that have caused you to mistrust His leadership.

2. Pull out a clean piece of paper and draw a timeline of your life. Start with your birth on one side of the page and draw an arrow going to the other side and write the date at the end to indicate where you are currently at in your life. Draw a vertical line at every point along the arrow each time there was a significant moment in your life, whether good or bad. Ask the Lord to reveal if any of these areas need further work in your heart or mind. Your willingness to have healing in these places will increase your capacity to trust and enable you to surrender your will in a greater way. (Note: If He doesn't say anything, don't worry! Remember He's the perfect guide and you don't need to go digging around for things if He doesn't reveal any.)

3. Put on some worship music and soak. "Soak" is a fun term we like to use for finding a comfortable place to sit or lay down, allowing the music and words to speak to you. It's not a time where you are worshiping or expressing yourself to God, but rather allowing Him to speak to you and minister to your spirit.

DAY 4
Hunger Cries

As Jesus went on from there, two blind men followed him, calling out, "Have mercy on us, Son of David!" When he had gone indoors, the blind men came to him, and he asked them, "Do you believe that I am able to do this?" "Yes, Lord," they replied. Then he touched their eyes and said, "According to your faith let it be done to you," and their sight was restored. Jesus warned them sternly, "See that no one knows about this." —Matthew 9:27–30

These last few days we've been talking about being led by the Holy Spirit, approaching Him and His Word with meekness, and allowing Him to be our tour guide in this life. However, I do want to illustrate that our will is not all bad! When its strength is fixed on achieving a goal or it exhibits itself as tenacious faith then the results are incredible! There are times when we put it to great use and the result is breakthrough and increase for us and glory for God.

I remember a time when I was watching a hero of mine on a television program. She said, "I believe I received more from the Lord just because I wasn't willing to give up. It was my sheer determination and willpower to get all that God said He had for me that allowed me to be here today." When she said this my spirit leapt inside of me. I understood what she was saying.

I'm reminded of two blind beggars in the Bible who had some serious willpower and determination — so much so that it landed them right in front of Jesus and ultimately, brought them their healing.

In the book of Matthew this story plays out. These two men were blind beggars who decided to follow Jesus one day. They were determined to get His attention, asking Him to have mercy and heal them. At first glance this story seems straightforward. It's not until you begin to unpack the original meaning that you begin to really get the picture of these men and the attitude in which they came to Jesus.

The word followed is a Greek word *akaloutheo*, which means "to follow after someone or something in a very determined and powerful manner." These men were not going to give up even if it looked hopeless. They would not be ignored! The way that they followed was key to their breakthrough. It took everything they possessed.

We also learn these men didn't just go quietly. Even in this verse it says that these men were crying out and yelling for Jesus to help them. The word "crying" is another Greek word kradzo, and it means to scream, yell, exclaim, or cry out at the top of one's voice.[4] I think we may be getting the picture here. These men were not going to give up. Spoiler alert: Jesus looks at them and says, *"according to your faith, you have been healed."* It was almost as if Jesus was saying, "Your faith was so persistent it could not be ignored!"

So, what does this have to do with the will? It was their will that made them persistent and kept them there, and their faith that made them well. If these men hadn't had a strong will to see and a determination to stay until they were healed, they may never have received what they came for.

I like to say, "Leaders aren't smarter, cuter or better. They just simply outlast the crowd." A strong will may be one of your greatest assets for the kingdom.

Annie!

---

4 Renner, Rick. *Sparkling Gems (Page 587) Published 2003. Print.*

MY PRAYER FOR TODAY

Jesus, I thank You that surrendering my will doesn't look like not having strength or determination. I thank you that you value my will so highly you gave it to me as a free gift. Thank you that when I use it to focus on the things you direct me to, it will bring GREAT results for Your kingdom. I ask You to lead me and urge me to get the very things You have promised. I want to be one who outlasts the crowd; one who is never satisfied living sick, broken or blind. I want to be in hot pursuit of You, believing You can do what You said You would do! I want to partner with You so I ask You to create a steadfast spirit within me. Keep me here! Help me to stand. Give me grace for the journey. I pray this in Jesus name! Amen.

MY CONFESSION FOR TODAY

I confess I've got a submitted and sanctified will. I've got my eye on the prize and I'm locking in. I'm not going to be discouraged, deterred, demoted or deferred. I'm an overcomer! I may not have my healing yet, but I'm in hot pursuit of the one true Healer. I will outlast the crowd because I have a spirit of perseverance. I'm going to get what I've come to get. Jesus is working all things for my good. I confess this in Jesus' name! Amen.

MY ACTION STEPS FOR TODAY

1. Take a moment and examine your pursuit of God. Have you wavered in following Him? Take a moment and rededicate your life back to Him.

2. Have you felt like having a strong will has been a negative thing when it comes to serving God? Have you felt misunderstood? Ask God to heal your perspective, forgive those who have misunderstood you, and show you what He had in mind when He made you.

3. Is there something you're asking God for right now? Could God say that your faith is getting His attention? If not, ask yourself how determined you are and whether you could engage your will to persist in your pursuit.

DAY 5
Tried, Tested and True

When your fathers tempted me, proved me, and saw my works forty years. — Hebrews 3:9

Have you ever found yourself in a difficult situation? That spot between a rock and a hard place? It seems like it doesn't take much time after making a decision to follow Christ before we come face to face with something hard in life. I remember facing my first heartbreak after serving God. I thought God was supposed to guard my heart and I was confused that I was in a situation that had caused so much pain and found myself having to grieve the loss of a relationship.

Now after years of serving God, I've walked through harder things. Loss of jobs, loved ones, struggles with physical health and even my mental health with depression and anxiety. The Bible says it rains on the just and the unjust. It seems as if no one is immune to it, not even the people of Israel. Can I get a witness?

When we read Hebrews 3:9, it's not hard to remember the Israelites' time in the desert. Yet the wording here is quite strange and rather intriguing. Why would they use the word tempted? The original Greek lets us in on it a little more. "Tempted" is the word **peiradzo**, and it's an old Greek word meaning "to put to the test; to test an object to see if its quality is as good as others have claimed, boasted, or advertised." It simply means wanting to try something out, after hearing about it for so long, to see if it's really as good as they have been saying.

Just like the Israelites, we sometimes find ourselves in a situation where our belief in God is tested to the fullest. In other words, in a place where we had the opportunity to see God demonstrate to us that He is who He says He is. He doesn't lie to us. In fact, He is the real deal and He did what He said He would do.

The verse goes on to say the children of Israel "proved" God. Proved is a Greek word taken from the word dokimadzo, which describes something that is authentic, reliable, approved, trustworthy and real.[5]

Moses didn't need to test or prove God. He had seen Him face to face but the Israelites were in a different place with God. They were learning about Him, they didn't know Him. Many times when we face hard times we get to encounter a part, or side of, God's nature in such a personal way that our knowledge about Him changes to knowing Him. Our own personal history with Him builds trust that no one can take away from us. And let's not forget our personal history with God proves His faithfulness and is the very thing that defeats the devil. Why else do you think God would want to build with us in such a deep and profound way?

MY PRAYER FOR TODAY
Jesus, thank You for Your faithfulness to me. Thank You that even in the moments of deep pain and times when I have felt I am in a wasteland, You have come in strength. You have come to prove Yourself to me. You have come to show me You are who You say You are. Let this truth lodge so deeply in my heart that it can never be uprooted. In those moments of testing and wondering, let me look for You. I want to build a history in You that is a firm foundation and a weapon against the enemy. Thank You for upholding me. Thank You for guiding me. Thank You for proving Yourself again and

---

5 Renner, Rick. Sparkling Gems (Page 595) Published 2003. Print.

again. I pray this in Jesus' name, Amen.

MY CONFESSION FOR TODAY

I confess that every trial I walk through is a proving ground of your goodness, faithfulness and truth. The very desert I've walked in will get to be the place where my knowledge about You becomes an encounter with You and the trustworthiness of Your nature. I reject the lie that You will not come through for me. You are who You say You are and You will do what You have promised You will do. Today may be a day of testing but tomorrow will be a day of proving. My God doesn't need my help to be strong and mighty. He is powerful! Today I believe God. Today I trust God. I confess this in Jesus' name, Amen.

MY ACTION STEPS FOR TODAY

1. If you are facing a hard situation or you have found yourself in a desert place, take a moment to ground yourself in the Word. Pull out Psalm 37:25 and put it to memory. Think about those words and meditate on it all day long. If you have time, read through the entire psalm and put first person language in as if you are making this declaration yourself.

2. Find a way to spend sometime outside today. Take a walk to the mailbox, take your coffee break out back or roll your window down during your drive. Try to find some silence. In this moment, ask God to speak to you. It could be a simple word or a clear thought, a warm feeling of His nearness or even an intuitive feeling that He's there.

3. Spend some time journaling your thoughts and prayers today. Write down some of the things you are asking God to show Himself strong in. Later on you will be able to turn back to see all the ways God kept His promises.

WEEK Two

ENGAGE YOUR MIND

Our mind is the prime real estate in our lives; the place where all of our battles are won and lost. Eventually, what we've been thinking about leads to actions and solidifies our lifestyle. Our minds are so powerful that when we lose them, we lose everything. If we have a renewed and edified mind, we live a peace-filled and God-intended life. It's really that simple!

The Bible has a Greek word for our "minds" used in the book of Thessalonians. The word is nous, which describes everything in the realm of the intellect, including one's will, emotions, and the ability to think, reason, and decide.

The good news is the enemy of our souls cannot read our minds. Let's not forget, the devil is not God's evil twin. He is not a god. He is a fallen angel with a God-complex. Being able to read and know the thoughts of men is an attribute God saved for Himself as the Godhead. He alone knows what you're thinking. He knows if your mind is racing out of control like a racecar on a speedway, and He knows if your mind is lying down and at rest. He knows the small victories and celebrates them with you. He also knows about those haunting thoughts you have and He wants to deliver you from them, never leaving you or forsaking you in them.

Your mind and thoughts are serious business to God. He knows that just like a seed turns to a seedling and a seedling turns into a full grown plant, your thoughts develop and grow over time. He understands the dangers, but also the possibilities of growing the right thought life. He intentionally helps us to work on our thought life, helping us to uproot any potential dangers.

In our daily life we may hear people say, "think good thoughts," or "a positive mind is a positive life." Although it's all pointing you towards having a better life, as followers of Christ we don't live from the outside in, but rather from the inside out. The Bible says we have been given the mind of Christ. So, this means we don't just try to think more positively or try to meditate and clear our minds. No! We have a heavenly gift, given to us by our Creator to help and assist us in this life on Earth. It's a whole mind. The mind of Christ is a sound mind. It's been given to you and your only responsibility is to receive and believe that it's yours. This belief will empower you along the journey to renew and transform your mind!

DAY 6
Trimming The Fat

Do not conform to the pattern of this world, but be transformed by the renewing of your mind. Then you will be able to test and approve what God's will is—his good, pleasing and perfect will. —Romans 12:2

Today we're going to look at one of the most foundational scriptures when it comes to renewing your mind. Turn in your Bibles to Romans and read chapter 12 verse 2. I love how the amplified version reads:

"Do not be conformed to this world (this age), [fashioned after and adapted to its external, superficial customs], but be transformed (changed) by the [entire] renewal of your mind [by its new ideals and its new attitude], so that you may prove [for yourselves] what is the good and acceptable and perfect will of God, even the thing which is good and acceptable and perfect [in His sight for you]."

The word "conformed" is the Greek word **suschematizo** which means "to fashion alike" or "the same pattern". What this verse is explaining is that we are to be completely different to the unbeliever. Where do we begin? It's very clear: THE MIND. Our thoughts, meditations and daydreams should look completely different from those who are not following Christ. Our mind should become like Jesus' mind, being fashioned like His, cut from the same pattern.

He gives us hope in all of this! He uses the word "transformed" which gives us an understanding of how this happens. This is another Greek word metamorphoo. You may recognize it — it is from the same word that we get the word "metamorphosis". It describes a comprehensive change, one so extensive it's like a caterpillar changing into a butterfly! Doesn't this give you hope? The fact is our minds are not changed immediately and our thoughts do not change overnight. However, if we apply God's Word to our lives, with faith in our hearts, it will happen over time. Our thoughts will begin to line up with His thoughts and our mind becomes renewed! It's only a matter of time. So much of what God does in us is not an immediate work, but a work that happens over time; requiring trust, obedience, reliance and perseverance. It's a relational work, not just a restorative effort. He wants to partner with us and teach us about Himself in the process.

I want to take it a bit further. Why do we need a renewed mind? It is not just for the world to see that we are different. Let's be honest, most of the world will never see what our minds see, and they will never know what we are thinking. Paul, the writer of Romans, gives us more insight into the benefits we will reap as we go to work renewing and morphing our thoughts into Christ-thoughts. He says it clearly at the end of the verse, *"...so that you may prove [for yourselves] what is the good and acceptable and perfect will of God."* The reason we renew our minds is so that we will understand and know the will of God for our lives. Think about it like trimming the fat off some meat; you want to keep what's good and get rid of what's unnecessary. A renewed mind is a mind that's clear and receptive to the will of God; a renewed mind can spot God's thoughts, God's ways, God's paths. Having the mind of Christ is one of your greatest keys to success, to your destiny, and to the purposes of God for your life.

Never underestimate what a renewed mind will do for you! When the days seem hard, and the thoughts seem challenging; when you have "that thought" which continues to plague you and you go after it, when you relentlessly put it under the authority of Jesus Christ, (I'll explain more of this in the next couple lessons) don't give up! This is the very key that unlocks the will of God in your life.

MY PRAYER TODAY

Jesus, I thank you that you never ask us to do something without having a complete picture of the benefit we will reap when we do it. I thank You that we don't just live a life to get by; You've given us a life so that we can thrive in Your will. I ask You to anoint my mind to see what You are doing. I ask You to teach me to take every thought captive. I will not give up! I will give in to the process of renewing my mind and knowing your will shall be my reward! I ask You to put a spirit of endurance in me. I make an agreement with You today. You are working in me and You are completing in me what You promised. I pray this in Jesus' name, Amen.

MY CONFESSION FOR TODAY

I confess I have the mind of Christ! My thoughts are turning into God thoughts. I may not have a completely renewed mind yet but I'm on my way. God's will is my reward and I'm getting exactly that. Today I'm taking every thought and aligning it with what God says about me. I am an overcomer. I can endure. I have strength because He has put strength within me. Today the will of God is becoming clearer to me because my mind is becoming cleaner. I have grace to think new thoughts, no matter how long I've been thinking this way. I can begin again and I am choosing to do that today!

I confess this in Jesus' name, Amen.

MY ACTION STEPS FOR TODAY

1. Take the verse from Romans 12:2 and write it out and/or highlight it in your Bible. Take some time to commit it to memory. Really allow it go down deep and become a part of your spiritual library.

2. Think about an area in your life where you need to know God's will. With this area in mind, ask God to help you set your thoughts on spiritual things this week. Consider taking a break from asking Him what He wants you to do and focus on getting your mind spiritually aligned. You might be surprised if your answer comes without looking for it!

3. Old patterns are hard to break. Set up a "reminder" system. Maybe a 30 minute alarm on your phone or a morning and evening routine. Take those moments to settle your thoughts and ask God to take you further in your journey of renewal. Ask Him for greater level of grace!

DAY 7

Make Up Your Mind

Now set your mind and heart to seek the LORD your God.
—*1 Chronicles 22:19*

What does it mean to actually set our minds on God? The Bible says, *"as a man thinks in his heart, so he is"* (see Proverbs 23:7). This means whatever you are thinking about is going to eventually show up in your actions. We can't help it! God made us to become like whatever we behold. The word "mind" in the Greek is the word *phroneo* meaning "to think, to consider, or to ponder." It carries the idea of intense reflection.[6] I've heard it said, "Your thought life is how you talk to yourself." When we go after having a renewed mind, we understand that what we think about, consider, or ponder throughout our day needs to change. Our "stinking thinking," as Joyce Meyer says, needs to stop. We can't renew our minds if we are not willing to take responsibility for our thought life. We can't always help what comes into our mind but we can control whether or not it stays there. By the power of the Holy Spirit working in us, we can change!

Let's take a quick look at what it means to make up our minds on things above as the Bible describes it (see Philippians 4:8). Have you ever stopped to consider that your mind has a mind of its own? We have to learn to set our minds. What do I mean by that? Just like it says, we have to take our thought life to a higher place. We have to settle into a comfortable place where we're actually reproducing healthy thoughts. It's like when you're learning to make bread — it takes practice to get it right, to get in the groove, so that the dough has just enough air with just enough strong gluten

---

6 Renner, Rick. *Sparkling Gems* (Page 19) Published 2003. Print.

strands. You can't knead it too much, but you also can't neglect the process either. Now, let's jump over to Matthew chapter 5 and look at a sermon called The Beatitudes spoken by Jesus. (Take a moment and read Chapter 5 verses 1–12.)

Let's explore this concept of making up our mind for a minute. Our daily thoughts may sound something like this: "I feel so helpless. Nothing seems to work out for me, and each time I try something new I fail." But when we read the words of Jesus, who said, *"Blessed are the poor for theirs is the kingdom of Heaven,"* we should really be talking to ourselves like this: "You might feel weak but you are not weak. Jesus said He has given you the kingdom, even if you are poor in spirit," or, "Everything in the kingdom is mine including power, might and a sound mind. Today I'm taking God up on that promise. I'm setting my mind on Him."

Let's look at another one: "Wow, I can't believe they would act like that? I'm so mad. I honestly don't even think they know God. If they did they couldn't possibly act like that." Allowing the Word to influence us would sound something like this: "I can't understand why they would act like that, but I'm choosing mercy today. God, You've been merciful to me and I'm not perfect. I'm not going to hold anyone to that standard because I'm not the judge of anyone else. Thank you for giving me a spirit of mercy and not a spirit of judgment. I bless them!"

Let's look at one more: "If that happens to me one more time, I'm going to lose it. I can't believe after all I've done, now it's this. Everyone is going to get a piece of my mind today. I don't care, I'm telling it like it is." Again, with the Word as our foundation, we might say, "God, you said if I keep my peace, I am a child of Yours. So soul, you will have peace today! You will not rule me and drag me around. I belong to God and I'm keeping my peace by the power of the Holy Spirit."

Does this make sense? You always get to choose your response because it's your responsibility, it falls within the boundaries of your personal yard. Don't let the lie that the enemy feeds you: "you are always going to be this way" or "you'll never think that way" stay in your mind. He is a liar and he knows if you start to change your mind, you will change your life and eventually your effectiveness in the Kingdom. You've probably heard me say, "It's time to take your thoughts to trial." Well, that's exactly what you need to do!

Let me be really honest with you. It's going to be very hard at first. Your mind has been running the show for a LONG time and it can be exhausting going after your thoughts. I suggest taking one thought at a time and begin to speak to it. If it's a lie, call it as it is. If it's a judgment, don't act like it's not. Be as honest as you can with yourself. Ask the Holy Spirit, whom God gave to you as a helper, to give you divine guidance to know how to bring these thoughts under the authority of Jesus Christ and renew your mind.

MY PRAYER TODAY
Lord, thank You for the promise of a renewed mind! I confess I need to start taking better care of my thoughts. I am really convicted by this and I'm asking You to help me shift my focus today. Help me take each thought to trial. I ask You to remind me that all authority in Heaven and on Earth are mine. I am not weak. Give me the strength and divine power to start to live this life You've given me on purpose. I believe You are helping me change by the power of Your Holy Spirit. You are helping me to set my mind on Kingdom living and be the person I'm called to be. I pray this in Jesus' name! Amen.

MY CONFESSION FOR TODAY

I declare that I can do all things through Christ who gives me strength! I'm using that power to renew my mind on a daily basis. I'm putting away thoughts that lead to death, depression and discouragement. I'm setting my mind on things above. I'm replacing bad thoughts with good, life-giving and life-altering thoughts! Enemy, I will not tolerate thoughts that lead to a lack of peace, joy and mercy. I'm giving myself over to the things of the Spirit. I'm living on purpose and I'm thinking on Christ. I confess God is doing a new thing in me. My mind will be renewed! I declare this by faith in Jesus' name!

MY ACTION STEPS FOR TODAY

1. The Lord asks us to love Him with all our heart, mind, soul and strength. Take a moment to pray and meditate on what it means to love Jesus with your entire mind. Inquire of the Holy Spirit to reveal and show you what that actually looks like. Ask Him to highlight the ways your mind is hindered from fully loving God today.

2. Declare with your mouth saying: "I will love You with my mind today, Lord!" Speaking and declaring things in faith, even though we might be weak, is not hypocrisy. When we speak it out, we're letting our Spirit speak. We are fixed to actually believe it and become empowered to do it.

3. One key to renewing the mind is having a renewed and edified spirit. If you have your prayer language, practice praying in the Spirit under your breath any moment you aren't speaking to someone else. If you don't pray in tongues, that's okay. Just pray from your spirit man and worship the Lord under your breath. When our minds are engaged in prayer we're less likely to wander mentally and are able to fill our minds with spiritual things.

DAY 8
The Good Receiver

Who has known the mind of the Lord so as to instruct him? But we have the mind of Christ. —1 Corinthians 2:16

God is always willing to give us good things! The Bible tells us He gives us good gifts, but we have to be willing to receive them (see Matthew 7:11). The reality is God gave His only Son so we could have every good thing given to us, for us. However, receiving from God is not always as easy as it sounds.

A few years back I remember really struggling with God. I was overwhelmed with what He was allowing to happen in my life. I was complaining about it and telling Him what I really thought (I'm sure you've never done that... HA!). I'll never forget His voice, gentle but stern, saying to me, "Havilah, true trust is believing my intentions toward you are always good." I was overcome with emotion. I began to weep, just feeling His kindness towards me. I understood in that moment that I had been questioning His intentions toward me. I felt like my mountain was too big for God to handle. I was not getting the breakthrough fast enough. My relationship with God was difficult because it lacked true trust and I was unaware of the reality of God's goodness to me. It was a wrong belief God wanted to uproot from my heart.

Today we are talking about receiving the mind of Christ and I want to ask you a question: How good are you at receiving from God? When it comes down to it, do you feel His movement in your heart and mind? It's really important that you dig deep and answer this question. Please know there is no wrong answer here.

As a minister for almost two decades, I regularly have individuals come to me and say, "I can't feel God. I know He's real but I can't seem to experience him." I see the pain, frustration and even resentment in their eyes. I think it's common to hear the church say things like, "Well, it's not about feelings. It's about faith." I do agree with that theology; that primarily God wants us to believe Him by faith. He doesn't want us to trust in our emotions because they can change minute by minute. On the other hand, I can't help but suggest that God, who is the Creator of our senses and emotions, has given them to us for a purpose. Usually, when we can't experience Him, the difficulty lies with us.

So, let's consider a few more questions: Do you feel distant from others in your life? When you are with others, do you still feel alone? Maybe the inability to feel that connection has to do with a part of your heart that needs inner healing. Maybe your ability to receive love and feel emotionally connected to others is more hindered than you realize. If you think this may be true for you, I would like you to stop reading in a moment and ask the Holy Spirit to help you.

Let me ask you something else: Do you recognize the presence of God in only one area of your life? Is your mind impacted by God while your heart has a hard time experiencing Him? Does your heart connect to Him but you have a hard time feeling His emotions towards you? It's hard to experience all of Him if only a portion of you is really attuned to Him. I hope you will begin to take time to ask God to open your mind in a greater way, or ask Him to open your heart to really feel Him and connect with Him. It's okay if you are only just beginning to understand this part of you. Take your time; it is vital.

MY ACTION STEPS FOR TODAY

Here is what I suggest: get with a small group of friends, your spouse, or best buddy. In the quietness of your time together, confess to them your need to receive from God in a greater way. If you are aware of a specific area, tell them. It might sound like: "I need to experience God in my heart. I understand all about Him but I need my heart to be open to Him in a greater way." Ask them to pray with you. Just sit together and begin to ask the Lord to open up your heart and increase your ability to receive. Begin to thank Him for the gift of His Son. Thank Him for the cross that made a way for you to come to Him. Then, as you sit there, allow what is inside come up and begin to release it to the Lord. If it's sin, confess it; if it's hurt, confess it; if it's mental, emotional or spiritual walls, confess it. Be as honest as you can! Ask Him to do what only He can do: open you up! Take your time. You can take ALL the time you need!

It's okay if nothing specifically happens at that moment. Don't let the enemy lie to you and tell you nothing happened. He knows that if you actually feel God in this area, your spiritual life is about to change. You've confessed it. You were honest. Now give the Holy Spirit time to work in you and with you. Listen to hear if He asks you to do something else to help bring greater release.

There was a man in the book of 2 Kings named Naaman. He was a very wealthy man and had all he needed in this life but he was stricken with leprosy. The maid living in his home told Naaman's wife about the prophet Elisha, explaining to her that if Naaman went to the prophet he would be healed. Naaman went at once with all his horses and chariots, but before he arrived at the prophet's house, Elisha sent word to him to go to the river and dip himself in the water seven times. Naaman was ticked off. He was so furious that he yelled at the messenger and turned in a rage to go home. But one of his servants suggested he actually do what the prophet asked. Naaman then went to the river and dipped seven times and at the final dip, the Bible says, his skin was like the skin of a child.

Maybe God is asking you to do something and you're ticked off. You don't understand why He is asking you to do it. Why do you have to be stuck? I would ask you, "Why not do it?" What if you are getting closer to the breakthrough you have believed for? What if your next step is the seventh time in the water? Are you willing to receive even if you don't understand fully? Maybe you need to hear the same words I did — "True trust is believing My intentions towards you are always good!"

MY PRAYER FOR TODAY

Lord, thank You for the promises I have in You. I've been given the mind of Christ. I'm receiving it now! Thank You that I don't have to live this life without experiencing You in my mind, in my heart and in my emotions. I ask You to expand my capacity to receive from You. I'm desperate for a fresh touch. Help me not to give up. Anoint my heart to trust in You and receive. I confess I'm helpless without You. Give me a deep desperation for the reality of You. I don't want to say I'm alive if I'm dead on the inside. Lord, have Your way in me. I pray this by faith in Jesus' precious name! Amen.

MY CONFESSION FOR TODAY

God, I confess I'm Yours and that I belong to You! I declare I have the mind of Christ. Your thoughts and emotions towards me are always good today and forever. I declare I'm leaning into Your heart and not turning back. I will not allow the enemy to lie and say I'll never feel or experience You fully. You are the keeper of my heart, mind and emotions and You have full access to all of me. I confess I need more of You. You are coming to my rescue. I receive Your thoughts today. You are expanding my capacity and anointing my heart. I declare this in the name of Jesus! Amen.

DAY 9
From Filthy To Flawless

Therefore put away all filthiness and rampant wickedness and receive with meekness the implanted word, which is able to save your souls.
—James 1:21

During our renewal process we really need to understand what is imperative to our growth. We can't possibly focus on every area of our spiritual walk at one time, so it's vital we know what the "big deals" are to God. The only way to ever really know is to look to the Word of God and to beware of assuming. James, in his book, explains two "big deals" to God. He begins in the first chapter at the twenty first verse by declaring we should put away all filthiness and wickedness. It's critical that we know exactly what it is that he's talking about so we aren't left guessing.

The Greek word for "filthiness" is the word *raparian* and it means "obnoxiously filthy".[7] Now jump forward to James 2 and read verses 1–7. Note the two different men he was talking about in the story. He was referring to two different groups of people in the church: one group being of nice appearance and the other group, filthy dirty. Reading verse 2 he says, *"For if a man wearing a gold ring and fine clothing comes into your assembly, and a poor man in shabby clothing also comes in..."*

Comparing James 1:21 and James 2:2 you will find the words "vile" and "filthiness" coming from the same Greek word. The Greek word raparian portrays a man whose body and clothes are so foul, the stench is evident to everyone around him. It literally takes their breath away!

---

7 Renner, Rick. *Sparkling Gems (Page 19)* Published 2003. Print.

This is exactly the word James uses to describe the bad attitudes of the believer. It stinks in such a way that everyone around us can smell it. It's like wearing a piece of clothing that is so filthy, it's impossible to get clean. When we have a negative, pessimistic, uncooperative, cynical or indifferent attitude, it just plain STINKS! And it's evident to those around us whether we admit it or not. It can't be ignored and we can literally drive people away from us!

When it comes to renewing our mind we have to be willing to be honest about our actions. When we see our actions or attitudes are not lining up with what the Word of God and the attitude of Jesus teach, we need to lay them aside. We need to take them off like a dirty piece of clothing. Let's look at this a little more.

"Lay aside" means to lay something down and to push it far away and beyond reach. It comes from the Greek word *apotithimi*. When we look at James 1:21 it's important to see that part of "putting off" or "laying aside" is not just removing the attitude, but pushing it far away. When James uses the same word, talking about dirty clothing and our bad attitudes, it's clear he's telling us, GET IT OFF!

When it comes to laying aside the attitudes of the mind, it's ALL about removing the filthy garments we've become accustomed to. Not just taking them off when we want to and then putting them back on, but removing them once and for all, throwing them out of reach! It's coming to a place where we decide to walk in meekness, giving ourselves over to God and the fruit of His Spirit. As we do this we begin casting off wrong thinking and picking up the new garments of the Spirit.

MY PRAYER FOR TODAY

Lord, I thank You for creating me to be fascinated by You; captivated in every way, including my mind and thoughts. Help me to first recognize the filthy things that I've allowed to influence my thoughts, which have caused a stink in my daydreams and mental life. I, in turn, replace them with eternal thoughts that lead me to see Your beauty and glory. Give me an increased grace to walk in the Spirit! I pray this in Jesus' name! Amen.

MY CONFESSION FOR TODAY

I will choose to guard my mind today. I will guard it from vile and filthy thoughts, and choose instead to think on God's beauty, splendor and glory. I was made for God. I was made to encounter and glorify Him through my thoughts. I will set my mind on things above today, seeking to have the words of my mouth and the meditations of my heart be pleasing to Him. I pray this in Jesus' name. Amen.

ACTION STEPS FOR TODAY

1. Identify an area that you struggle in; an area where you see your flesh has a habit of winning the battle. Choose a close friend and ask them to hold you accountable in this area; especially over the next week or two. Keep this area before the Lord during this time as well and evaluate after one or two weeks. Do you see any changes?

2. Consider this analogy: You're incredibly thirsty and need a refreshing drink of water but the only water available has been contaminated with just one small drop of poison. You're not going to drink it right? We wouldn't put the smallest bit of poison into our bodies even if we were incredibly thirsty, right? Think about all the potential ways you're allowing small drops of poison into your mind and know that if left unaddressed, they will eventually lead to a mind given over to filthiness.

3. Identify and make a list of the three most influential ways you allow filth into your mind and way of thinking. Once you have this list, counter it with three solutions or commitments to fight against them. Ask the Lord to help you overcome these ways of thinking so that you can live freely and wholly unto God with a clean mind.

DAY 10
Cleaning Up

For God has not given us a spirit of fear, but of power and of love and of a sound mind. —2 Timothy 1:7

Have you ever felt like you're losing your mind? Have you ever thought you might be going crazy? If you have, you are not alone. The mind is very powerful! Even in the Bible there was a man of God who thought he might be losing his mind, and in his most difficult time he wrote the words, **"God has not given us a spirit of fear; but of power, and of love, and of a sound mind"** (2 Timothy 1:7).

Paul wrote these words during a very tumultuous time for the early church. The Roman Emperor, Nero, was becoming more and more insane and persecuting the church daily. Timothy was now a pastor of the Ephesian church, and he knew that if Nero's secret police could kill him, they would enjoy doing it. You can imagine why Paul would write these words under the power of the Holy Spirit. The great Comforter was speaking life into Timothy's spirit. You can clearly see why Paul would write, **"God has not given us a spirit of fear,"** but I love that he went on to say, **"but of power, and of love, and of sound mind."** I want to focus on "sound mind" as we complete our week's homework on renewing the mind.

What does it mean to have a sound mind? The phrase "sound mind" comes from two Greek words **sodzo** and **phroneo**. Sodzo means "saved" or "delivered". It suggests the idea of a person who was on the verge of death but then was revived and resuscitated because of new life breathed into him. Phroneo carries the idea of a person's intelligence or frame of thinking; including his rationale, logic, and emotions. It refers to every part of the human mind, including all the processes that are engaged in making the mind function and its ability to come to good conclusions. Together, the words give us a picture of a mind that has been delivered, rescued, revived, salvaged and protected and is now able to come to rightly conclusions.[8]

It's important to realize that the Bible does not ignore the fact that fear will come; feelings of weakness or feelings of being unloved. Even feeling that we might have an unstable mind are possible. God confronts this foreboding fear and says, "It's not of Me! I'm coming to heal your mind. I'm coming to empower you!" The Bible also says that perfect love casts out fear. Simply speaking, if there is fear, it's not of God. But, if it's there, how do we get it out? How do we achieve a renewed mind?

One way we renew our minds is to ask God for HELP. We ask Him for something we can't do for ourselves. We come to Him in the meekness we talked about earlier, and we ask Him for the power of His Spirit to stabilize, revive, salvage and protect our mind; to make it new.

Can God heal our minds? Yes! He has the power to deal with any destructive force that comes our way. Sometimes it's an instantaneous (miracle) work, and sometimes it's a process (healing) that takes time. Either way, God is faithful! The question should not be, "Is He able?" but rather, "Will I let him?"

If you're anything like me you can walk around for a long time thinking that life is great and you are the queen of it (just below Jesus, of course! *wink*), and then in a moment, the rug gets pulled out from under your throne (maybe your precious baby fell out of the shopping cart at Target, or maybe you accidentally sped past a cop in a school zone,

8 Renner, Rick, Sparkling Gems (Page 73) Published 2003. Print.

or someone you love dearly got rushed to the hospital) and you think "REALLY?!" It is in these moments when we feel as though we're dangling over a cliff edge by a piece of dental floss when the thoughts that have been shaping our hearts and minds will come to the surface. If you're spending ten hours a day on Facebook and five minutes in God's Word, don't be surprised when you don't have a holy reaction to the stress that life brings.

Romans 12:1–2 is too good to paraphrase on this point:

"I beseech you therefore, brethren, by the mercies of God, that you present your bodies a living sacrifice, holy, acceptable to God, which is your reasonable service. And do not be conformed to this world, but be transformed by the renewing of your mind, that you may prove what is that good and acceptable and perfect will of God."

Did you realize that the we, the Church, God's girls and guys, YOU and me, are called to prove to the earth what God's perfect will is? How does Paul suggest that we live in such a way? By being transformed by the renewing of our minds! We've talked about heart renewal and now we have the desire for a sound mind. And this is how we get it: 1. Ask God to heal our minds, and 2. Take action to renew our minds. Every day. In God's Word and by His Spirit. You and I can have a clean and sound mind as we allow all of our thinking to be filtered through the water of the Word (see Ephesians 5:26).

MY PRAYER FOR TODAY

Lord, thank You for the power of Your Word! I understand You want to renew my mind making it clear and sound. I ask You to continue to help me take every thought captive and place it under the authority of God. I ask You to come and stabilize my thoughts! Help me drink deep of Your Word on a daily basis, allowing it to truly wash and transform my mind.

I pray this in Jesus' name! Amen.

MY CONFESSION FOR TODAY

I know that I have the power to make choices that will lead me towards or away from having a sound mind, free of fear and torment. I will set my heart to be aware of these opportunities and make choices that direct me to grow in faith rather than in fear. I will stand on the eternal truth of scripture and continue to allow its truth to change my way of thinking until it changes the way I respond. I declare this in Jesus' Name! Amen.

MY ACTION STEPS FOR TODAY

1. Recognize how many situations you came across today where fear was your initial feeling. How many were there? I think it's first important to realize how frequently we deal with fear or tormenting thoughts on a daily basis without even recognizing it.

2. When you recognize a situation that produces anxiety, fear or torment, stop and talk to the Holy Spirit. Speak to your own spirit too by reciting these scriptures, regarding fear, out loud. There truly is power in speaking out the Word of God.

ENGAGE YOUR WORDS

Scientifically and psychologically, it is said that what you speak over yourself has more impact on you than the daily, positive things that other people say about you. The Bible has been saying this long before this data was ever available. God's Word does not lie! When we confess and agree with what God is saying over us, there is supernatural power in it!

Proverbs 18:21 tells us, *"Death and life are in the power of the tongue."* Even if you have heard this many times the meaning could easily get lost without looking into the original Greek. The Greek word for death is maveth which means dying and the Greek word for life is chay which means living. The actual meaning is that your tongue; what you say holds the ability to release life or deliver death. It also means that the words that are spoken continue to live on until they are interrupted. That is how important what we say or confess can be; IT IS POWERFUL!

The Power of agreement is another way we get to partner with God to bring about transformation. The defining moment comes when our hearts begin to agree with what we believe and we declare it. Once we believe something and begin to confess it, it's as good as done. The Bible says, *"If you declare with your mouth, "Jesus is Lord," and believe in your heart that God raised Him from the dead, you will be saved."* Wow! Did you catch that? Confession and belief is in our DNA. It's a powerful weapon! It's the key to our spiritual redemption or it could be our spiritual death.

Lastly, the scripture is very clear that what's happening on the inside is eventually going to show up on the outside. Jesus said in the book of Luke, *"...out of the abundance of the heart [the] mouth speaks."* A critical heart produces a critical word and a loving heart produces a loving word. If you have an unbelieving heart your words will be full of doubt and a self-righteous heart will have words of arrogance and haughtiness. But a kindhearted person's words will drip with grace and love; words which soothe the very soul. The melody of a heart of compassion will sound like songs of empathy and care. The simple ingredients to a powerful life are found in the things we hold in our heart making their way out of our mouth and shaping our reality.

DAY 11
Owning It

Let us hold fast the profession of our faith without wavering;
(for he is faithful that promised;) —*Hebrews 10:23*

As a minister's kid, one of the most frequent questions I'm asked is, "How did you learn to have your own walk with the Lord?" Honestly, in my younger years, it was frustrating! For various reasons, but predominantly because I never felt that I had a really dramatic or extreme conversion. You see, growing up, I lived in an evangelist's home. I would spend day after day, night after night, meeting after meeting, hearing about my Dad's radical salvation. He would tell stories of walking into a church as an atheist and coming out filled with the Holy Spirit, ready to change the world. So, when someone would ask me about my conversion, I would sheepishly explain that I just believed from a young age. It wasn't until I started having my own life experiences that I began to know God for myself and then I understood that my unique story was just as exciting. I wasn't living my Dad's life, I was living my own story with God. In His mercy, God takes every man and woman to a place Oswald Chambers calls, "the great divide," where what we hear finally becomes our reality, what we understand becomes a great faith, and we form our own personal convictions. It's a different journey for each one of us, but no less real.

In Hebrews 10:23, the Bible explains this process well. Take a look at the phrase, **"Let us hold fast the profession of our faith."** Let's look at the word "profession." It comes from the Greek word homo and it means one of the very same kind. The second part of the word is logos meaning word. Together the words are homologia meaning "to say the same thing," or so it seems until you look a little deeper. In the King James Version the word homologia translates as "profession" too. So, to really understand the meaning of the word you have to look at the word logos, or words. Let me illustrate and then we'll come back to this point.[9]

As many of you know, I'm a public speaker. I spend time preparing messages and then share everything — my thoughts, convictions, and beliefs — with all types of different people. My words are what I believe, and what I think. They are what I've expressed. They are, in essence, me! Let's say you have listened to me, you've heard my heart and my thoughts. You agree with me, maybe even quote me on occasion, but perhaps you're not really changed by them. Now, the next time you hear me — after I declare my convictions and my beliefs — you feel connected. You agree and you find yourself inspired, or emotionally moved. At this point, you might say we are becoming aligned. We are aligning in our thinking and beliefs. Once you've repeatedly heard my words, agreed with them, and they have gone into your heart, you might come to embrace them, and allow yourself to be transformed by them. They will start to become your own words and convictions. All of a sudden they won't be 'Havilah's" words any more, they will be yours! You will have a strong conviction about them and begin to express them, even to the point of not referencing me any more.

When you look at the word homologia in other Scriptures, you will see that it's not talking about someone who just states something they've heard, repeating it or regurgitating it. It's an individual who has heard the words, embraced them and has finally made them their own. When we as believers begin to live a homologia life we begin to experience radical change. When we read the Bible over and over, listening to the words God uses and embracing them in

9 Renner, Rick. Sparkling Gems (Page 314) Published 2003. Print.

our 'inner being'[10], they finally begin to be our words. It's our God who can accomplish it. It's the Holy Spirit who is at work in us, but He needs us to read and absorb the words first.

So, when this believer begins to open her mouth to confess something, the words aren't empty any more. It's from her very core! She is no longer talking for someone else or repeating another. They are her words, her beliefs, and her heart. "Real confessions are made out of words from God that have been sown into the heart. After a period of meditating and renewing the mind, you finally begin to see it the way that God sees it. You really believe what God believes! And from that place of heartfelt conviction, you then begin to speak and declare your faith!"[11] Now I'm no longer embarrassed to talk about my conversion. I've come to understand that Christ died for me. I was a sinner saved by grace, and even though I may not have been what the world deems a "bad sinner," I am a sinner and my sin alone was enough to put Jesus on the cross. His love for me took Him to the cross to die for me and His blood shed that day guarantees me a place in eternity!

The reason I can say this with such conviction in my heart is that as I've heard and studied the Word of God I've agreed with it and aligned myself with it. I've spent so much time immersing myself in it that it has become my own truth, my reality. The Bible is about me! I am who it says I am, and I can do what it says I can do.

So, with that reality, my confessions are not empty words or hopeful thoughts, and yours don't have to be either. As His Word becomes truth in your life, your confessions will change. How you live will change! You will begin to feel empowered to truly live out your God-given destiny. Your hope will build! The peace that God said you could have, you will have. Isn't that exciting? Praise God!

---

10 Psalm 51:6
11 Renner, Rick. Sparkling Gems (Page 179) Published 2003. Print.

MY PRAYER FOR TODAY

Lord, thank You for the power of Your Word! Thank You that it's alive and changing me. I ask, as I listen to the Word, that I would begin to agree with it. Let it go so deep inside so that it becomes part of me, shaping my convictions and belief system. I ask that as I seek to know You that Your Word would become me! Give me the power to make Your words my confession. I pray this in Jesus name! Amen.

MY CONFESSION FOR TODAY

I confess the Word of God is living and active in me. I'm hearing the Word and making an agreement with it each time I do. It's going deep inside of me and changing me from the inside out. As I read the word, I'm listening to it — taking it in — chewing on every morsel. It's slowly becoming my words and my convictions. My profession is not just something I'm repeating. I'm declaring it and it's becoming me! I have the mind of Christ. I have the Word of Christ in me and it's coming out of my mouth. I declare this by faith in Jesus' name! Amen.

MY ACTION STEPS FOR TODAY

1. Speak out and repeat back to the Lord as you read the Word today. Pick a few passages that fill your spirit and say them out loud, allowing them to penetrate your mind and heart. Repetition causes us to start to believe, and remember the truth that may be weak within our hearts.

2. Read Revelation chapter 4. Repeat it over and over several times, allowing it to speak to you. Notice the repetition and descriptions used. Consider if there are many more layers to the scripture than you're experiencing. Ask the Lord to continue taking you deeper into His word, revealing the hidden mysteries as you speak it, read it, study it, pray it and do it often. His Word is a shoreless ocean of much treasure!

DAY 12
The Good In You

That the sharing of your faith may become effective by the acknowledgment of every good thing which is in you in Christ Jesus.
—Philemon. 1:6

Have you ever stopped to listen to what your mouth is actually saying? Do your words line up with the Word of God, which you profess? Have you activated truth by the confession of your mouth?

Paul said we need to say good things about ourselves. In Philemon 1:6 he prayed, *"that the sharing of your faith may become effective by the acknowledgment of every good thing which is in you in Christ Jesus."* Let's take a closer look at what he was talking about. Why would Paul use the phrase "become effective?" Paul is saying here that it's possible to cultivate God's blessing on your life not just by acknowledging it in your mind, but by declaring it with your mouth. God has done amazing things for you, but just because He did it doesn't guarantee its activation. Just because a car has an engine with the potential to drive, it doesn't mean it can do so without a key to activate it. It's still a car, but it's inactive!

The word "effective" is the Greek word energo and it's where we get the word energy. But in this particular verse it carries a different idea; the idea of something that has suddenly become energized or activated.[12] Understanding this means the verse could be translated, "that the sharing of your faith may become energizing and activated." Let's go back to the car example. A car has huge potential but if it's never turned

---

12 Renner, Rick. *Sparkling Gems* (Page 59) Published 2003. Print.

on, it's just a hunk of metal. The moment the key is put in the ignition its potential radically changes. This is like many Christians — they are filled with potential. Think about it! If God said all things are possible with Him, then we are sitting on huge possibilities! We are not hindered by age, ethnicity, gender or talent. In fact, God loves to use the simple things to confound the wise. But there are keys to igniting our potential, and Paul is trying to give us a key!

In Philemon 1:6, Paul speaks about, *"every good thing which is in you in Christ Jesus."* Think of all He has done for you! He healed you, saved you, delivered you, redeemed you and protected you. He's given you a new heart, a sound mind and gifts and talents personally assigned for you to use for Him. You have tons of potential! But are you activated? You may struggle with feeling useless. You might battle thoughts of worthlessness, but you are not worthless. You just need to be activated! Paul says the key to activation is confession. So, what are you confessing about yourself? What are you declaring over your future? What have you decided to stop complaining about and start believing God for?

One last thought for you: I know sometimes in the body of Christ personality has a lot to do with who is seen as a leader. The person who can talk the loudest is the most heard, the most dominant is the most seen, etc. but this is not the case when it comes to the spirit world. In God's eyes, we're all on level ground and He does not see certain people as leaders and others as followers. To Him, all of us are leaders, and each of us have the potential to be great. He asks each of us to acknowledge ourselves as we truly are and confess good things about ourselves. He says that we each have the key to ignite God's goodness in our lives if we start to confess it.

MY PRAYER FOR TODAY

Lord, thank You for Your Word! Thank You that it's helping me to become the person I'm called to be. I ask You today to help me. I ask You to begin to fill my mouth with words of life about my future. I confess I've not always used my mouth for good things. I've complained about how You've made me and what's happened in my life. Help me to put a stop to it today. Holy Spirit, I'm asking You to remind me when I begin to use my mouth to complain or speak negatively. Gently nudge me to stop. Help me to turn it around and begin to thank You for all you've done and all You are going to do. I pray that I will begin to activate the potential that You see in me. Help me to believe that You are powerful enough to do what You said You would do.

I pray this in Jesus' Name! Amen.

MY CONFESSION FOR TODAY

I declare I'm going to use my mouth for good today! I'm going to confess the good things You have done for me and the good things You are going to do. I'm going to activate my faith by verbalizing Your goodness. I will not make excuses about why I'm inactive. I will take personal responsibility for what fills my mouth. I'm going to change because You said it's possible. I'm not going to listen to the enemy about what my natural eyes see. I'm going to use my spiritual eyes to see in the spirit, to declare truth and to speak life. I'm not always going to be this way, I'm changing and I'm using my potential!

I declare this in Jesus' Name!

MY ACTION STEPS FOR TODAY

1. Take some time to repent for using your mouth for negative things. Sometimes we can have a stronghold in a particular area and for a lot of people it is the mouth! We are used to using our mouths in a negative way and it's hard to imagine not ever doing it again. Ask Jesus for help. Ask Him to deliver you from any ungodly habit you have slipped into. Ask Him to prompt you to change it as you go through your day.

2. Today, each time you hear yourself use your mouth for negative things I want to you to quietly take responsibility. In your heart ask the Lord to forgive you. If you can say it out loud, do it! Ask Him to forgive you. Tell Him you are serious about changing and speak something positive — either about yourself or someone else.

3. If you have spoken negatively about something or someone with someone else today I want you to ask their forgiveness. Go to them and say something like, "I wanted to ask your forgiveness for what I said today. I'm really trying to work on my words and what fills my mouth. I said some things I'm not proud of and I want to change." The next time you are tempted to speak in haste, you might think twice if you know you'll have to go back and make it right!

DAY 13
Talk With Your Mouth Full

Therefore, confess your sins to one another and pray for one another, that you may be healed. The prayer of a righteous person has great power as it is working. —James 5:16 (ESV)

A couple of years back I was struck with a strange condition. Each time I prepared to speak publicly I was overcome by a violent illness. I got extremely sick to my stomach — sick enough to be in the bathroom throwing up just moments before I was about to speak. I couldn't figure out what was going on. It came on suddenly and without warning, causing me huge concern. I went to the doctor who carried out some tests, ultrasound, and blood work. Finally, in a state of bewilderment, I confessed to a friend what had been going on. He recommended I call a mutual friend of ours who had a gift of discernment. I called him that night.

I began talking to him and explaining what had been happening to me. He asked me questions as the Holy Spirit led him. Finally he asked me about a particular instance that the Lord was showing Him prophetically that I had experienced years before. At that moment the Holy Spirit reminded me of a time when I was in someone's office and they had spoken some damaging words over me. I began to cry as I remembered what was said, and how I had made an agreement unknowingly with them (remember that the enemy doesn't have to speak blatant lies for us to agree with him). As my heart was gently exposed, I began to confess and repent for allowing my heart to make an agreement with that lie. I withdrew the statement I had made back then and God's Spirit washed over my broken heart. The agreement I had made was broken once and for all. I was free from it and my mysterious illness never struck again.

When it comes to confessing to one another, it's important we understand the way the enemy works. He loves darkness. He loves us to keep things hidden in secret, so that he can feed us shameful thoughts, full of condemnation. Our only defense is to bring it out into the open so that the Holy Spirit can then lead us to freedom. The word "confess" in James 5:16 is the Greek word ekzomologeo, and it means "to declare, to say out loud, to exclaim, to divulge or to blurt it out." I love that it means to blurt it out!

I can think of many times when I was under the conviction of the Holy Spirit and I had the courage to 'blurt it out'. When it comes to nurturing ourselves, we must think of this as a crucial part of the process. It may seem counter-productive for some people, or a little taboo, like talking with your mouth full, but God says that as we confess our faults, we invite restoration.

I love how the Amplified Bible puts it: it clarifies your sins to be, *"... your faults, your slips, your false steps, your offenses."* Well, that seems to cover it all! Did you know that the word "faults" is the Greek word paraptoma meaning a failing in some area of one's life? One Greek translator says it can also denote a person who accidentally bumped into something, or one who had accidentally swerved or turned amiss and has thus thought something or done something that is erroneous. I really enjoy this definition because sometimes our faults are a simple failing in an area or an accident. Don't get me wrong — I don't think people just accidentally fall into sin. But sometimes we can hurt ourselves without being totally aware, just like I did in that office long ago. I wasn't consciously thinking that I would make an agreement against the Word of God, but in the moment I faced a decision of fear or faith, and I chose fear. However, once it was brought to my attention, I renounced it at once, confessing 'my faults' and repenting before the Lord and also my friend in Christ.

We need to get good at using our mouths to confess. I think of how many arguments I've been in that don't end with the words, "I was wrong, will you forgive me?" Sometimes it's implied, as though the offended party should just know. But I think it's important to admit what we did and to make it right. More importantly, God considers it important too, and He created us! He knows what's best for us and confession (and the freedom it ushers into our lives) is a part of that.

PRAYER FOR TODAY
Lord, You are so faithful to me! What an amazing God You are, that You can forgive and release me from the sin and stain of this world! Today, I ask You to help me. I confess there are areas in my life that need some serious change. I first need courage to be honest, courage to bring it out in the open so I can be healed. I now understand the enemy is at work to try and keep me silent so that sin can hide in me. I will not allow it, and I will not allow him to torment me any longer. I do not belong to him anymore! I belong to You! I understand I have failed but I am not a failure. Please help me to live the life you died to give me! I pray this in Your precious name, Jesus. Amen!

CONFESSION FOR TODAY
I have the mind of Christ! When I choose God in my life, my mouth is filled with the things of God. I can confess truth! I'm declaring I will not hide things in my life. I will not allow the enemy to torment my mind by lying to me and saying I'll never be free. I will sin, but I am saved by grace; grace that allows me to be honest about my faults, needs and sins. I belong to God! He is not afraid to hear about my sin. I'm not disappointing Him when I confess sin. He made a way for me to be healed and confession is a part of that. I declare I'm forgiven and cleansed. I can walk with my head held high because I'm a child of God.I declare this by faith in Jesus' name! Amen.

MY ACTION STEPS FOR TODAY

So, what now? Do you have something you need to confess? Is it so deep inside you thought you'd never let it out but you need to? Is it causing you pain? I have a few suggestions for you:

1. Ask the Lord what needs to be confessed. Unloading for the sake of unloading is not what we are talking about. It's important to ask God for the things that need confessing and to come in a spirit of wisdom, freedom and truth.

2. Find a safe friend. It could be a spouse, a leader or a best buddy, just someone who will keep it confidential and someone you feel safe with. Take time to explain to the person how vital it is that they keep your privacy.

3. Confess! Yes, it's that simple. Remember that all the details are not what's important, only what you feel you need to share. Be honest. Talk about what was going on in your heart. What your motives were. It's about a heart cleanse, not just about facts or details.

4. Pray together. Take time to ask the Lord for help. Confess your need for Him but also ask for forgiveness. It might sound like, "Lord, I was wrong. Please forgive me." Let the cleansing power of forgiveness wash over you!

5. Take all the time you need! If you need to pray for a while, that's great. If you need to talk about it for a while, great. But I want to remind you that God does not need a lengthy process in order to forgive and release. He is all-knowing, all-powerful and is able to hear the heart.

DAY 14
Feed Others

And let us consider one another in order to stir up love and good works, not forsaking the assembling of ourselves together, as is the manner of some, but exhorting one another, and so much the more as you see the Day approaching. —*Hebrews 10:24–25*

In the ancient Greek world, military leaders often would gather their troops together to exhort them. They would explain the painful reality of war, but they would also explain the glory of winning a major victory.

"Exhort," in the Bible, is the Greek word parakaleo. It's the combination of para meaning "alongside" and kaleo meaning "to call, to beckon, or to speak to someone." Together it means someone who is right alongside of a person, urging him, beseeching him, begging him to make some kind of right decision.[13]

This is what we are called to do as believers. We are called to exhort one another. In fact, the Bible challenges us not to forsake or neglect being with those who encourage us in the faith to stand strong. When it comes to life and the battles we face, the Bible also says we should exhort one another daily. Encouraging one another that the battle will eventually be won if we fight hard, stand strong and forge ahead, never giving up or giving in to the enemy of our soul.

Exhortation can also come from the Holy Spirit. He wants to use our mouths to exhort one another. Our mouths can be used for all kinds of things but one of its greatest abilities is to call forth faith, declaring the things of God and speaking against the lies of the enemy.

---

13 Renner, Rick. *Sparkling Gems* (Page 26) Published 2003. Print.

I want to encourage you with a thought: When you come upon someone who is discouraged, overwhelmed, or disheartened, do you just give them empathy or do you give them something more? I think it's vital we learn to exhort others in the Spirit by challenging them to rise above, reminding them that the fight is long and hard, but it's not over and we will win if we faint not.

Exhorting may sound like this to someone you know: "I know you are having a hard time, but I also want to remind you that there is a real enemy who wants to discourage you. You are in a battle but you were made to fight. God loves you and He sees you. He has a call on your life. You are not weak even if you feel like you are. You can do hard things because God said you can. He said you can do it through Him who gives you strength. Can I pray with you and ask God to help you?" We don't have to force feed others but we can acknowledge and exhort others in the faith.

For those of us who have been walking with the Lord a long time, it can almost be difficult to receive exhortation from others. We may already be in the practice of exhorting others, but when a need arises in our own hearts for this gift, we shrink back. Sometimes I think to myself, "I should be stronger than that." Other times I think I am above needing encouragement, when in reality no one alive and breathing on this earth is above needing it. God created us with needs so that He can fill them. If this is speaking to you, I encourage you to learn how to draw out exhortation from those around you. Don't necessarily go and ask everyone if what you're doing is right or wrong but go and ask your friends what they are learning from God today. And listen carefully for anything that you might need to hear. They just may say something that will spark a spirit of encouragement in you that you would not have received if you weren't looking for it!

MY PRAYER FOR TODAY

Lord, thank You for the gift of exhortation. Thank You that the Holy Spirit lives inside of me and is exhorting me each day. He is explaining the war at hand, how to deal with the hardships and the hope of true victory. I ask You for grace to walk in a spirit of exhortation. I ask You to point out others along my path that may be discouraged, overwhelmed and feeling like giving up. Give me the words to say. Help me not just empathize with them but exhort them in Christ. Help me to stay in relationship with others who are willing to exhort me in love. Give me courage to face my fears and not hide from the battle.

I pray this in Jesus' name! Amen.

MY CONFESSION FOR TODAY
I confess I have the Holy Spirit in me! He's working in me and exhorting me daily in truth. I am not weak. I have the Spirit of God in me helping me to do hard things. I am not alone but I'm surrounding myself with other believers who are exhorting me towards righteousness. When I feel alone, isolated or depressed I'm going to get help. I'm going to find a community that encourages others in love, exhorting them in the faith. I'm not going to wait for others to find me and find out how I'm doing. I'm going to show up like a grown up and stay in relationship.

I confess this in Jesus' name! Amen.

MY ACTION STEPS FOR TODAY

1. Find someone you know who needs to be exhorted and find a way to help them. Leave a voicemail or send an email or card in the mail. Call them up and explain what you have been learning. Tell them the Lord put them on your heart and ask if you can pray with them. Be courageous! You don't have to be a church leader to minister to others and you don't have to be a pastor to lovingly share the truth.

2. Ask the Lord to soften your heart to receive exhortation. If you are reminded of a time someone tried to exhort you and you drew back, ask the Holy Spirit why you reacted this way. Let Him lead you to truth!

3. Practice! I know this is going to sound funny but I want you to practice what you are going to say when someone comes to you in need of encouragement. Sometimes in the midst of the moment we resort right back to our old pattern. The only way to change what we do is to practice something new. Role play what you would say and how you would say it. Ask the Holy Spirit for the right thing to interject! (I think of my dad who always says, "Let's pray about that.")

DAY 15
Talk Like God

Therefore be imitators of God, as beloved children. —*Ephesians 5:1*

Have you ever had a situation where you had to exchange your immediate behavior? Maybe you were talking angrily to your kids, and as soon as the phone rang you switched to your happy voice? Or maybe you were in an argument with your spouse and someone came to the door and you immediately lowered your voice and changed its tone? Or have you been angry but didn't want someone to know so you quickly slapped on a smile?

It happens all the time! We're confronted daily with situations where we simply have to act right. Let me ask you a few more questions to make the point: Have you ever met someone you really admired and found yourself trying to imitate them? Were you so taken by them that you wanted to do exactly what they were doing?

Pull out your Bible and read Ephesians 5:1. Doesn't Apostle Paul ask us to do this very thing? He says, *"Therefore be imitators of God, as beloved children."* The word is a Greek word mimetes, which means to imitate someone or to mimic what you see someone else doing. It's used to describe actors or performing artists who acted on a stage for their profession. It frequently depicts modeling after a parent, teacher, champion or hero.[14]

I think it's great to have personal heroes, but it's really important to have heroes in the faith — men and women who have gone before us! I cut my spiritual teeth reading books by Kathryn Kuhlman, Benny Hinn, Tim Story and

---

14 Renner, Rick. *Sparkling Gems* (Page 137) Published 2003. Print.

Oswald Chambers. As I grew in my faith, I read books by Joyce Meyer, T.D. Jakes, Bill Johnson and many others. I've found tremendous hope in their stories, receiving endless revelation and priceless wisdom. It's crucial that we learn from others. God esteems peoples' journeys of faith so much that He devoted a whole chapter in Hebrews to them. In fact, many times the passage in Hebrews 11 is referred to as "The Hall of Faith." Stories of mighty men and women who, through faith, did great historical exploits.

So, who do you imitate in your life? Do you have a personal hero? Are you taken with people who know God, talk like Him, and walk like Him? What captures your fascination? Does God? I would suggest if you are not fascinated with God it's not because He's not fascinating. The lack of perspective always lies within us.

I want us to look at a few more verses in the Bible to see where else the Greek word *mimetes* is used.

MY ACTION STEPS FOR TODAY
Turn to 2 Thessalonians 3:7–9 and write it down here:

Now underline the word follow/imitate. I want you to notice what Paul is asking of the Thessalonians: for them to imitate him! It could be translated, "It would behoove you to follow our example— imitate and mimic, with the goal of replication, the things you observe in our lives."

2. Let's do it again! Turn to Hebrews 13:7 and write it down here:

Now underline the word follow/imitate (consider) in the verse. It could be translated, "You need to carefully model your faith after theirs — doing what they do, saying what they say, acting like they act — considering the great maturity and fruit produced by their lives."

What all these verses communicate and what Paul is imploring the reader to do is to ACT LIKE GOD! Yes, like a professional actor who hones his craft. It's going to take effort, anticipation and premeditated action to be like God. Your heroes in the faith didn't imitate the characteristics of God by accident, and neither will you. It's an intentional, motivated response!

One last thought: practice, practice, practice! It's going to take a ton of effort and a ton of time to be like God, but it will be worth it. Paul knew it would take a ton of practice as well. Let's go back to the beginning of the verse to see how he starts out. The phrase, "therefore be" translates the Greek word ginesthe and it's meaning translates the verse as "constantly in the process of becoming." So, my question is, are you in the process of becoming? Have you decided to take captive your unsanctified thoughts, emotions, feelings and behaviors and surrender them to God? Have you decided to show up like a grown up and begin to act like the person God wants you to be?

MY PRAYER FOR TODAY

Lord, thank You for the promise that I can do all things through You because You are strengthening me. I confess I'm convicted today by the thought that I need to act more like You. I really want to be like You. I want to act more like You in my everyday life and lead others to You. I am asking for the power of Your Spirit to empower me to live this life You've called me to. Lord, I want to live in such a way that I can say to others "follow me like I follow Christ." Give me spiritual heroes in the faith! I ask for spiritual men and women that I can look to for guidance and examples.

I pray this in Jesus' name! Amen.

MY CONFESSION FOR TODAY

I confess I'm going to act like God! I was created to live and exemplify His life in this world and I'm going to do it. Enemy, I have listened to you for far too long. I'm not stuck like this and I'm not always going to act like this. God is anointing my thoughts, emotions, feelings and behavior to look like Him. He is giving me clarity to live like Him. I'm going to start acting right! I understand that God is asking me to act like Him and I'm going to do it! I confess I'm changing. God is giving me the ways to act that lead me to life and lead others to life as well. I can do this!

I confess this in Jesus name! Amen.

WEEK FOUR

ENGAGE YOUR ENEMY

When it comes to defeating our enemy T.D. Jakes said it best, "You must understand your enemy, for you cannot defeat what you do not understand." Let's be honest. most of the church is a bit split on the subject. There are various camps in the body of Christ. One would lean towards never recognizing any demonic activity. If by chance someone happens to "act out" in their presence they would have a designated driver to help navigate that person to deliverance. Preferably behind closed doors and without a lot of attention. Then there are other groups where it's here a devil, there a devil, everywhere a devil devil. Everything is. 'the devil is hindering me' or 'the devil's really attacking me.' It's a full on battle!

It's very important to understand what the Bible says when it comes to the enemy of our souls. It keeps us grounded in the fight and without fear. One of the most foundational and telling passages is found in John 10:10 where it says, "The thief comes only to steal and kill and destroy. I came that they may have life and have it abundantly."

Let's dive in and look at the Greek to find out the true meaning. The word thief is the Greek word klepto which means to steal. It's where we get the word kleptomania or kleptomaniac! It also contains the word embezzler, meaning to convert fraudulently for ones own use. or a pickpocket who is so artful in the way he steals that his exploits of thievery are nearly undetectable.[15] We can begin to see what the enemy's true character is like. He loves to get his hands on what we possess. If we have joy — he wants it! If we have freedom — he's coming after it! But he doesn't just come right out and ask for it. He doesn't just grab it in large quantities. No! He slowly and artfully takes our treasure, our identity, our purity, our freedom, until one day we turn around and it's all gone. He has robbed us!

Now if we are smart and have caught on to His ways, we will see he is a thief and will not allow this. But the verse goes on to explain another way he hurts us. The word 'kill' does not mean death here. No, the word 'kill' in the Greek is the word thuo, which means to sacrifice.[16] The devil doesn't have to TAKE from us... He just needs us to believe his lie long enough that what we are missing is worth sacrificing ALL we have. A bowl of soup was all Esau needed to give up his future! (Gen. 25) We have all done it at one time or another. We may have given away our bodies for a moment of gratification, our dignity for a moment of inclusion, our conviction for a moment of entertainment, our character for a moment of satisfaction, our ministries for a moment of fame, our marriage for a moment of thrill. The devil doesn't always have to steal because most of the church is giving it away already!

---

15 Renner, Rick. Sparkling Gems (Page 547) Published 2003. Print.
16 Renner, Rick. Sparkling Gems (Page 547) Published 2003. Print.

DAY 16
Resist Him

Submit yourselves therefore to God. Resist the devil, and he will flee from you. —James 4:7, ESV

At the age of 19, I found chapter four of the book of James. Or maybe I should say it found me! I would read it over and over again at every chance I could get, pondering what it meant to submit to God and resist the devil. I imagined myself with my small little frame and loud voice, paralyzing the enemy. I even prepared a message on James 4:7, explaining my seemingly huge revelation, which I would speak when I traveled to little churches up the California coast. As a young follower of Jesus, I loved the thought of knowing I was in a battle. I was zealous, passionate, and ready for a good fight. I cried as I read stories about Joan of Arc and her courageous mission to free France. If you've never studied her life, it's worth your time.

It wasn't until many years later that I realized it was going to take all I had to engage, or more often, stay engaged, in this battle. I came to understand I was in a battle whether I liked it or not. God had been fighting long before I ever understood or even knew Him. This battle was going to take all I had but, like every good fight, there is something to be won. God hadn't put me on this Earth to helplessly stay out of harm's way; rather, I am His co-heir, His partner in the struggle. He is my comrade. He is your comrade too. He wants to help us simply by giving us every tool needed not only to strike our adversary, but also to defeat him and keep him under our feet.

Let's re-read our focus verse for today. The word "resist" comes from the two Greek words *anti* and *istimi*. Anti means against, as to oppose something. The word *istimi* means "to stand". Together, it becomes *anthistemi*, which means "to stand against" or "to stand in opposition". This word demonstrates the attitude of one who is fiercely opposed to something, and therefore determines that he will do everything within his power to resist it, to stand against it, and to defy its operation.[17]

Doctors have prescribed to patients antihistamines for years. It's a type of drug which helps in blocking the receptors of histamine. In the same way when we resist the Devil we begin to have a blocking agent were we are no longer receptive to his influence. We have a divine agency working within us that makes us immune to his impact or his effect.

I love how James uses this word to help us understand our attitude when it comes to resisting the devil. Passivity, apathy, and denial will never set us free from the schemes of our enemy. It will only leave us vulnerable, which will lead to exhaustion, and finally defeat — barely getting by and never experiencing true victory.

I'll never forget what the Holy Spirit said to me one day as I was struggling with feeling vulnerable, weak, and insignificant: "It's time to take yourself seriously, because I do." It struck me like a baseball bat to the head.

The word for devil is a compound of the words dia and balos. The word dia means "through", as to pierce something from one side all the way through the other side. The word balos means "to throw", like to throw a ball, a rock, or some other object. These words joined together mean to repetitiously throw something — striking again and again and again until the object being struck has finally been completely perpetrated.[18]

---

17 Renner, Rick. *Sparkling Gems (Page 942) Published 2003. Print.*
18 Renner, Rick. *Sparkling Gems (Page 604) Published 2003. Print.*

Can you see how the devil comes against you? Do you feel him attacking you in one area over and over again until you finally give in or give up? He comes again and again until he finally wins. Like we've talked about, he is an opportunist. He's not all knowing, but he's relentless. Have you ever said to yourself, "If that happens again, I couldn't take it," or "If I have to go through that one more time, I don't know what I would do"? I believe these are the moments he is waiting for — times of weakness where we make agreements contrary to the Word of God.

Not so long ago, I found myself saying, "You know what I can't handle? I can't handle being wrongly accused." It wasn't more than a week later that I was caught right in the middle of unfounded accusations. I was a wreck! I couldn't understand what had happened and I was dumbfounded. After getting off the phone with the person who was accusing me, I felt the Holy Spirit gently remind me of my words. At that moment, I broke under the conviction of the Spirit and asked God to forgive me for making that kind of declaration over myself and making an agreement with this accusation. I had given the enemy an entry point into my life.

Lastly, let's look at the word "flee." The word flee in the Greek is so exciting! It is from the word pheugo, which from the earliest times of Greek literature meant to flee or to take flight. It was used to depict a lawbreaker who flees in terror from a nation where he broke the law. The reason he flees so quickly is that he wants to escape the prosecution process.[19]

I love this! The devil knows he is a lawbreaker. He knows he has no authority over a believer in Jesus Christ. When we use the name of Jesus and the Word of God against him, he has no power. Did you hear that? He can't do a thing. Not only does he lack any authority, but if he stays there, he will eventually be ruled and even dominated. He has to flee!

---

19 Renner, Rick. *Sparkling Gems* (Page 617) Published 2003. Print.

An expanded interpretation of James 4:7 could read:

"Stand firmly against the devil! That's right — be unbending and unyielding in the way you resist him so that he knows he is up against a serious contender. If you'll take this kind of stand against him, he will tuck his tail and run like a criminal who knows the day of prosecution is upon him. Once you start resisting him, he'll flee from you in terror!"

MY ACTION STEPS FOR TODAY

1. Take out a piece of paper and write down the five to ten lies the enemy speaks over you.

2. Go to the end of this lesson and circle the ten Scriptures that corresponds with the lie you have believed.

3. Pick one Scripture you are going to memorize this week.

Write it down here:

MY PRAYER FOR TODAY

Lord, thank You for giving me the power of Your Name and Your Word. I understand I have not been fully using them as You've intended me to. I choose to use them today to stand against the devil and all his schemes. Devil, I will no longer allow you to have free access to my mind and emotions. Get ready to flee. I am standing up to resist you. I intend to persecute you with the full authority of God's Word! In the

name of Jesus, I command you to leave my mind alone.
I will no longer ignore, write off, or give-in to your lies. I do
not belong to you. I belong to Jesus and I'm partnering with
Him today.

I pray this in Jesus' precious name. Amen!

MY CONFESSION FOR TODAY
I confess I am not a weak person! I have the power of
God, the name of Jesus Christ and the Word of God at my
fingertips. When I choose to step in to my full authority as a
believer, my enemy the devil must take flight. I will no longer
allow the devil to torment, shame or harass my mind. Devil, I
do not belong to you, I belong to Jesus. I'm coming after you.
I'm taking every thought captive and if it doesn't align with
the Word of God, it's getting kicked out. I'm on a mission to
renew my mind until it comes under the authority of Jesus
Christ and if you stay there you will too.

I declare this by faith in Jesus' name!

100 THINGS THE BIBLE SAYS ABOUT ME[20]
1. God has expressed His kindness to me *(Ephesians 2:7)*
2. God's power works through me *(Ephesians 3:7)*
3. I am a citizen of Heaven *(Philippians 3:20)*
4. I am a dwelling for the Holy Spirit *(Ephesians 2:22)*
5. I am a holy temple *(Ephesians 2:21; 1 Corinthians 6:19)*
6. I am a light in the world *(Matthew 5:14)*
7. I am a light to others, and can exhibit goodness, righteousness and truth *(Ephesians 5:8–9)*
8. I am a member of Christ's Body *(1 Corinthians 12:27)*
9. I am a member of God's household *(Ephesians 2:19)*
10. I am a minister of reconciliation *(2 Corinthians 5:17–20)*

---

20 http://teachingsundayschool.blogspot.com/2010/02/100-things-bible-says-about-me.html

11. I am a new creation *(2 Corinthians 5:17)*

12. I am a personal witness of Jesus Christ *(Acts 1:8)*

13. I am a saint *(Ephesians 1:18)*

14. I am adopted as His child *(Ephesians 1:5)*

15. I am alive with Christ *(Ephesians 2:5)*

16. I am assured all things work together for good *(Romans 8:28)*

17. I am blameless *(I Corinthians 1:8)*

18. I am blessed in the Heavenly realms with every spiritual blessing *(Ephesians 1:3)*

19. I am born again *(I Peter 1:23)*

20. I am born of God and the evil one cannot touch me *(1 John 5:18)*

21. I am chosen and dearly loved *(Colossians 3:12)*

22. I am chosen before the creation of the world *(Ephesians 1:4, 11)*

23. I am Christ's friend *(John 15:15)*

24. I am completed by God *(Ephesians 3:19)*

25. I am confident that God will perfect the work He has begun in me *(Philippians 1:6)*

26. I am crucified with Christ *(Galatians 2:20)*

27. I am dead to sin *(Romans 1:12)*

28. I am delivered *(Colossians 1:13)*

29. I am faithful *(Ephesians 1:1)*

30. I am forgiven *(Ephesians 1:8; Colossians 1:14)*

31. I am given God's glorious grace lavishly and without restriction *(Ephesians 1:5,8)*

32. I am God's child *(John 1:12)*

33. I am God's coworker *(2 Corinthians 6:1)*

34. I am God's workmanship *(Ephesians 2:10)*

35. I am growing *(Colossians 2:7)*

36. I am healed from sin *(I Peter 2:24)*

37. I am hidden with Christ in God *(Colossians 3:3)*

38. I am His disciple *(John 13:15)*

39. I am holy and blameless *(Ephesians 1:4)*

40. I am in Him *(Ephesians 1:7; 1 Corinthians 1:30)*

41. I am included *(Ephesians 1:13)*

42. I am more than a conqueror *(Romans 8:37)*

43. I am no longer condemned *(Romans 8:1, 2)*

44. I am not alone *(Hebrews 13:5)*

45. I am not helpless *(Philippians 4:13)*

46. I am not in want *(Philippians 4:19)*

47. I am overcoming *(I John 4:4)*

48. I am part of God's kingdom *(Revelation 1:6)*

49. I am persevering *(Philippians 3:14)*

50. I am prayed for by Jesus Christ *(John 17:20–23)*

51. I am promised a full life *(John 10:10)*

52. I am promised eternal life *(John 6:47)*

53. I am protected *(John 10:28)*

54. I am qualified to share in His inheritance *(Colossians 1:12)*

55. I am raised up with Christ
    (Ephesians 2:6; Colossians 2:12)

56. I am redeemed from the curse of the Law
    (Galatians 3:13)

57. I am safe *(I John 5:18)*

58. I am the salt and light of the Earth *(Matthew 5:13–14)*

59. I am sealed with the promised Holy Spirit
(Ephesians 1:13)

60. I am seated with Christ in the Heavenly realms
(Ephesians 2:6)

61. I am secure *(Ephesians 2:20)*

62. I am set free *(Romans 8:2; John 8:32)*

63. I am the righteousness of God *(2 Corinthians 5:21)*

64. I am united with other believers *(John 17:20–23)*

65. I am victorious *(1 Corinthians 15:57)*

66. I am victorious *(I John 5:4)*

67. I belong to God *(1 Corinthians 6:20)*

68. I can approach God with freedom and confidence
(Ephesians 3:12)

69. I can be certain of God's truths and the lifestyle which He
has called me to *(Ephesians 4:17)*

70. I can be humble, gentle, patient and lovingly tolerant of
others *(Ephesians 4:2)*

71. I can be kind and compassionate to others
(Ephesians 4:32)

72. I can be strong *(Ephesians 6:10)*

73. I can bring glory to God *(Ephesians 3:21)*

74. I can forgive others *(Ephesians 4:32)*

75. I can give thanks for everything *(Ephesians 5:20)*

76. I can grasp how wide, long, high and deep Christ's love is
(Ephesians 3:18)

77. I can have a new attitude and a new lifestyle
(Ephesians 4:21–32)

78. I can honor God through marriage *(Ephesians 5:22–33)*

79. I can mature spiritually *(Ephesians 4:15)*

80. I can parent my children with composure *(Ephesians 6:4)*

81. I can stand firm in the day of evil *(Ephesians 6:13)*

82. I can understand what God's will is *(Ephesians 5:17)*

83. I don't have to always have my own agenda
    (Ephesians 5:21)

84. I have access to the Father *(Ephesians 2:18)*

85. I have been brought near to God through Christ's blood
    (Ephesians 2:13)

86. I have been called *(Ephesians 4:1; 2Ti 1:9)*

87. I have been chosen and God desires me to bear fruit
    (John 15:1,5)

88. I have been established, anointed and sealed by God
    (2 Corinthians 1:21–22)

89. I have been justified *(Romans 5:1)*

90. I have been shown the incomparable riches of God's
    grace *(Ephesians 2:7)*

91. I have God's power *(Ephesians 6:10)*

92. I have hope *(Ephesians 1:12)*

93. I have not been given a spirit of fear, but of power,
    love and self-discipline *(2 Timothy 1:7)*

94. I have peace *(Ephesians 2:14)*

95. I have purpose *(Ephesians 1:9 & 3:11)*

96. I have redemption *(Ephesians 1:8)*

97. I know there is a purpose for my sufferings
    (Ephesians 3:13)

98. I possess the mind of Christ *(I Corinthians 2:16)*

99. I share in the promise of Christ Jesus *(Ephesians 3:6)*

100. My heart and mind is protected with God's peace
    (Philippians 4:7)

DAY 17
Fight Him

And take... the sword of the Spirit, which is the word of God.
— *Ephesians 6:17*

Have you ever been accused of something and found yourself fumbling for words, struggling for the right thing to combat the accusation? This really is a picture of many believers today. The enemy throws out accusations, hurling them at us and we struggle with what to say, many times because what is being said is true. Remember, the enemy will not throw out a lie that is obvious, but more often stretches the truth. He gives us something to sink our teeth into, and once we have agreed with one thing it's easier to agree with a whole bunch of things. But God knows this, and like every good Father He has prepared a way of escape. He has prepared the exact weapon for the battle we are in.

One of the primary exercises of a Roman soldier was sword fighting. Each soldier was submerged in a strict daily habit of practicing his swordsmanship. He was given various objects to help him prepare for battle. One object in particular was the buckler, woven with willow branches, that was two times heavier than the one used in actual battle. He was also given a wooden sword two times the weight of an actual sword. This constant discipline and cultivation was essential for what lay ahead.

The soldier's primary training was to hit the enemy at his weakest point, to leave his opponent helpless, leaving him without a chance to respond or retaliate. He was taught to stab and not to cut, giving a fatal blow. Understanding this background will help us grasp what Paul is trying to teach in this passage below.

Let's read Ephesians 6:17 together: *"And take ... the sword of the Spirit, which is the word of God."*

When we see the phrase "word of God" in the Bible we can assume it has one of two meanings. One particular word is rhema meaning "a quickened, specific word from the Spirit."[21] The other is logos which is "the written word of God."[22] Lean in, this is where it gets good. Right here Paul uses the word rhema, he doesn't use the word logos. It's very powerful! Why? If Paul had used the word logos he would have been talking about a sweeping stroke against the enemy. But this would never do in battle! The Word of God in the logos term is always powerful, wonderful and active but it's not the weapon we need in the middle of a battle. We need a rhema word. We need the Word of God which is a specific, quickened word from the Scripture, placed into our hearts and hands by the Holy Spirit. We require a rhema word that gives us the ability not to run around slashing at our enemy, but to stab him at his weakest point and defeat him.

Having a hunt and peck experience where you flip through your Bible and stab aimlessly hoping God gives you a Scripture is not the appropriate thing to do when we are being lied about, stolen from, and destroyed emotionally and physically. We need the rhema word that has the power to expose the devil as the enemy he is and call him out.

In this instance we can think of the logos word as the double-weighted sword which the soldier used daily for strength and endurance training. We must train our minds and hearts daily in the full counsel of God's Word so that in the heat of the battle we are not stammering and defenseless. When the Holy Spirit wants to give us a rhema word, he pulls from the stock of Scriptures written on our hearts through daily

---

21 Renner, Rick. *Sparkling Gems* (Page 78) Published 2003. Print.
22 Renner, Rick. *Sparkling Gems* (Page 584) Published 2003. Print.

devotion. We know God's Spirit through His Word (logos) and when we know His Word, His Spirit can breathe life through it (rhema) in the greatest moments of need.

Vegetius, a Roman military expert, recorded in his history of the Roman army, all that was needed to kill an enemy was a mere two inch penetration.[23] This is a perfect picture of what the rhema word does! It helps us see our enemy for what he is.

A great example in the Bible is in Luke 4:3–13 when Jesus was in the desert with the devil. Jesus had been fasting for forty days and he was hungry and tired. I'm sure we could all just imagine — Satan comes to Him and begins to attack Him, throwing temptations right in His face. How does Jesus respond? He doesn't just yell, "Get away Satan. Stop bugging me!" He specifically addressed him with a rhema word. After Satan tempted Jesus with food, Jesus drew the sword that the Holy Spirit put in His hand (a rhema word) and said, *"...It is written, 'Man shall not live by bread alone, but by every word of God'"* (vs. 4). To this stabbing sword of the Spirit, the enemy had no response.

Then Satan offered Jesus all the kingdoms of the world if He would just bow down and worship Him. Jesus is given a deep, penetrating word (a rhema word) from the Holy Spirit that left Satan with no answer. Jesus replies, *"You shall worship the LORD your God, and Him only you shall serve"* (vs. 8).

Lastly, Satan makes a final attempt at defeating Jesus by asking Him to prove that He is God. Jesus replies, "It has been said, 'You shall not tempt the LORD your God'" (vs. 12). With one final stab, Jesus penetrates Satan and, almost fatally wounded, the devil flees from the scene!

---

23 Renner, Rick. *Sparkling Gems* (Page 584) Published 2003. Print.

When I read this passage I can't help but have a mental picture of what was happening in the Spirit. Can't you just see Satan trying everything he has to trip up Jesus? I'm sure there was a smirk on His face. His eyes sparkled with the joy of hoping to finally conquer the Son of God. But as he throws these words at Jesus, congratulating himself inwardly, Jesus has a co-laborer. Even in His physical weakness Jesus reaches His hand behind Him and quietly and quickly grabs the sword (a rhema word) that the Holy Spirit had gently laid in His hand. He then thrusts it forward taking Satan's breath away with each blow. I love this! Jesus never loses power, even in His physical weakness.

Let this be a picture for you today. Understand that whatever the enemy throws your way, God wants to give you a rhema word for the moment. And because of your diligent daily pursuit of His word, you will know it is Him when He speaks.

MY PRAYER FOR TODAY
Lord, thank You for giving me the sword (rhema) of the Spirit as part of my arsenal to defeat the devil. I now understand that You have given me a rhema word for each situation I face. I am not powerless, speechless or weak. I'm a daughter of God! I'm learning to listen to Your voice and use the weapons You have given me. Today, I'm living with intention to be the person I'm called to be, set apart for Your will and mighty through You. Please quicken my heart to Your voice today!

I pray this in Jesus' name! Amen.

MY CONFESSION FOR TODAY
I confess I belong to Jesus! He is helping me live for Him and defeat the devil. When the enemy comes to sidetrack, accuse, condemn or shame me, I have the sword of the Spirit to cut him off and shut him up. The Holy Spirit is empowering me to know what to say and what to pray at the moment of weakness. I'm not wandering around waving my sword hoping to defeat the enemy, but I have the sword (rhema) at my disposal to penetrate the devil. I'm more than a conqueror in Jesus Christ and greater is He that is in me, than he that is in the world.

I declare this by faith in Jesus' name! Amen.

MY ACTION STEPS FOR TODAY
1. Take a moment and consider different times when God spoke a rhema word to you about a situation or a relationship. Did it help? How did it change your life and/ or the situation?

2. Be prepared to receive a rhema word today! Take a moment to read the above prayer out loud. Slowly. Give time for the words to sink in to your heart and connect to your faith. Now make the confession. Say it loud and clear! Let the enemy know that today is not the day to mess with you!

3. Call a close friend and pray together. Please be courageous! Ask God to strengthen each of you by clarifying His voice. Confess your need to use the sword of the Spirit (rhema and logos) with greater discipline in your daily life. Be as open and honest as you can!

DAY 18
Empower Yourself

Finally, my brethren, be strong in the Lord and in the power of His might. —Ephesians 6:10

Pull out your Bible and turn with me to Ephesians 1. I want you to read the first 13 verses and each time you see the word "in" I want you to note it (if it were me, I'd circle it). How many did you get? I hope you came up with nine different times. In verses 3, 4, 6, 7, 10 (twice), 11, and 13 (twice), Paul says we are in Him, in Christ, or in the Beloved. Translated, this means we have been actually placed inside Jesus Christ. He has become our realm of existence and the place of our habitation. It means that even though you live on the earth, according to the spirit realm you live in Christ. It's really important that you understand this so that you get my next point. If you live in Christ, then you have access to everything He does. The same power that lives in Him is residing in you! Paul straight out says it in Ephesians chapter 1. Jump down to verses 19 and 20. Go ahead and read it out loud! Listen to yourself say the words.

Did you hear that? "...exceeding greatness of His power towards us who believe!" The King James Version reverses the order from the original Greek. The Greek says, "according to the power of His might."

Let's take a closer look at what "power" means here in our text. The word "power" is taken from the Greek word kratos, and it describes a demonstrative power. It means that it's not just a power that we think about or can imagine but it's actual power with demonstration.[24] It's not a hypothetical power but power that comes with an outward manifestation

---

24 Renner, Rick. *Sparkling Gems (Page 347)* Published 2003. Print.

— one we can actually see with our own eyes. The reason I noted the difference in Biblical versions above is because it's the identical phrase used in Ephesians 6:10: "power of His might." With that understanding we see that the same power that raised Jesus from the dead is the same power residing in us, or rather that we are residing in. What does this have to do with spending time with God? I want to possibly help alter your perspective of meeting with Him.

Many times as a young believer I would be in situations where I was asked to go have a "quiet time" with the Lord. They would send us off with our Bibles, journals, and pens for an hour or so to "go meet with God." Early on I began to really struggle with this. I lacked understanding of how to really meet with God. Was He supposed to come down and sit with me? Would He talk so I could actually hear Him? What was I supposed to journal about? Can you feel the pain I went through with all the questions in my brain?

Theologically, we are never 'not meeting' with God. He is always with us! With the perspective of the text above, we are living in Him. The Bible actually says, "in Him we live and move and have our being" (see Acts 17:28). He is using everything, and yes, I mean everything, to teach us about Himself and how we are to live in Him. I've been known to say, "I'm trying to meet God between the washer and the dryer." I think it's so important we understand that God did not come down so He could meet with us for one hour a day. He came to meet with us throughout the day! There is nothing wrong with setting aside time to read His Word and listen to His voice, but it does not replace the continual conversation happening daily, hourly, minute by minute. A friend of mine once explained that she leaves her Bible open throughout the day in her home to remind her that the conversation is still going. I love this picture! Learning about Him and learning how to abide in Him (see John 15:4) are two different things.

Let's look at Ephesians 6:10 again. I really like how the Amplified version of the Bible translates it: "In conclusion, be strong in the Lord [be empowered through your union with Him]; draw your strength from Him [that strength which His boundless might provides]." Note where it says, "be empowered through your union with Him." Our union, our relationship should bear demonstrative power. This means when we are seeking Him there should be a noticeable change. Not because we are mustering up change, but because we can't help but be influenced. I love the phrase "you become what you behold" and I think it's fitting here.

Let's remember that today it's all about spiritual warfare and part of spiritual protection is staying close to Christ. Jesus said in John 17 verse 12, "While I was with them, I protected them and kept them safe by that Name you gave me." His role and His nature are to protect us. When we choose to abide in Him we come under the covering of His loving hand.

MY PRAYER TODAY
Lord, thank You for loving me enough to allow me to hide myself in You and live there. Thank You for the protection that comes from being with You. I understand living in You gives me power and that power is tangible and active. Help me activate my faith to live in that power! I ask You to help me continue the conversation, moment by moment. I ask You to anoint my heart to love You and abide in You. Jesus, I want to know what it means to be found in You and found in Your might. I ask You to help tune my spiritual ears to hear Your voice and live in the fullness of a spiritual relationship.

I pray this in Jesus' name! Amen.

MY CONFESSION FOR TODAY

I confess that demonstrative power flows through me! I am abiding in Christ and He is abiding in me. I am His! I understand that as I live in Christ He has made available a tangible power to operate through me to others. I confess I am more than a conqueror in Christ! I am not weak and far away from God but I am living smack dab in Jesus Christ. He died so I can live in and live out the abundant life. I may not be fully who I want to be yet, but I'm on my way. I'm learning to live in Christ so He can live through me.

I declare this by faith in Jesus' name!

MY ACTION STEPS FOR TODAY

1. Take your Bible and place it somewhere where you can keep it open throughout the day. As you place it there, ask the Lord to anoint your heart to keep the conversation going.

2. If you were asked to give a testimony about God's tangible power working through you, what would you talk about?

3. Take a moment and write down one thing that keeps you from keeping the conversation going. Is it too much noise? Absorbing entertainment? Distracted thinking? A lack of divine peace? Now repent and let God help you overcome this area. Practice keeping the conversation with God going throughout your day. It will make a big difference in your walk with God, and you will see tangible results.

DAY 19
Suit Up

Put on the full armor of God, so that you can take your stand against the devil's schemes. — *Ephesians 6:11*

(Please open your Bible to Ephesians 6 and read verses 10-20 before we begin our study.)

Have you ever been discouraged by your failure to feel protected from the attacks of the enemy? Many times I've been surprised at how subtle, mischievous and downright vicious he is. Let me remind you that the enemy wants everything. He is territorial and his desire is to take everything you have, chew you up and spit you out. He is a liar, a thief and a murderer. Never forget you are in a battle until you are in Jesus' arms. Until then, engage in the battle; get your back off the wall and stand in victory.

Jesus knew as He left this earth we would need a ton of protection — so much so that He promised to send a Comforter to help us. He knew we would need it! But He also asked us to be very careful and put on spiritual protection specifically designed to help us.

In the passage above Paul says we need to "put on" our armor. This is where he clearly points to our responsibility to put on the protection Jesus has provided. The phrase "whole armor" is the word panoplia and refers to a Roman soldier fully dressed from head to toe.[25]

Let's take a look at what specifically we are instructed to put on.

---

25 Renner, Rick. *Sparkling Gems* (Page 319) Published 2003. Print.

LOIN BELT

In Ephesians 6:14 Paul tells us we have the loin belt of truth and to stand firm in it. The loin belt is the central piece of weaponry that holds almost all of the armor in its proper place. What Paul is referring to when He says "loin belt of truth" is the Word of God! If we stand firm in truth (Word of God) we can be confident that all the other facets of our armor will stay in their proper places.

BREASTPLATE

In the same verse, Paul explains that we have the breastplate of righteousness. The breastplate was specifically designed to cover the heart and the central organs. It's the most vital of all the armor. Righteousness means right standing with God. Do you see how important it is to protect your heart? God is basically saying to put on the understanding that you are standing right with Him. It will protect your spiritual life! Proverbs 4:23 says that we are to watch over our heart because out of it flow the springs of life. Understanding that God the Father sees you as righteous is vital to understanding how to walk before Him and keep your heart from offense.

SHIELD

In Ephesians 6:16, Paul declares that as a believer, you are specially outfitted with a "shield of faith, with which you can extinguish all the flaming darts of the evil one." A Roman soldier had a shield that was long, door-shaped, and covered in leather hide. He would take time to oil it every day to keep it soft and flexible. In doing this, anytime an arrow would hit the shield it would slip off and fall to the ground, never penetrating the armor. Our faith is meant to be cared for! We are to take it out (figuratively) and look at it, making sure it's well oiled so when the evil one comes to hit us with a fiery arrow it falls to the ground. Many times in the Bible oil represents the Holy Spirit. I'm strongly suggesting our faith be bathed in the activity of the Holy Spirit. He (the Holy Spirit) keeps our faith secure and prepared for attack!

SHOES
Amidst Paul's encouragement for us to be dressed for battle, he makes the assumption that our steps are already being guided by what the gospel of peace says: "Having shod your feet with the preparation of the gospel of peace." It's like he throws this in there, assuming we are already preparing appropriately. Shoes refer to where and how we walk. Get this — if we don't prepare our feet to walk in peace, PLAN DECIDEDLY to walk in peace, we will automatically walk into confusion. If the enemy can't get into your mind through your thoughts, he will try to trip you up with where and how you walk.

HELMET
In Ephesians 6:17, Paul talks about our helmet of salvation. In Roman times a soldier was given a helmet that was specifically made for him. It was sculpted metal, molded just for his head. When Paul tells us to put on the helmet of salvation I believe he is talking about taking personal responsibility to acknowledge your own salvation. It's the understanding that God saved you personally that protects our minds from the evil one. One of the greatest dangers is when we expect to be protected under someone else's salvation experience (mother, father, best friend, etc.). In this case, the enemy is sure to deceive us and mess with our minds. But, when we have been saved and we acknowledge Christ's Lordship in our own personal lives, it shuns doubt and protects our heads (thoughts) from the evil one.

SWORD

In Ephesians 6:17, we are taught by Paul that every believer has a sword and it's a sword of the Spirit, which is the Word of God. Remembering our previous teaching about Roman swords in battle, we understood them to be long daggers intended to be used in close battle. It was absolutely the most important tool to overcoming the adversary. I love this! In the book of Revelation we are told that we defeat the enemy by the word of our testimony and the blood of the Lamb (see Revelation 12:11). The word of our testimony is our personal experience in the Word being used as a weapon in our lives to overcome darkness and sin.

MY PRAYER TODAY

Lord, thank You for the incredible protection of a spiritual armor You have designed specifically for me. I thank You that I am given everything I need to defeat the enemy and live a victorious life. I ask You to anoint my heart for self-discovery. I want to stop being thrown around by the enemy, constantly being hit with his fiery arrows. I'm not called to just get by, I'm called to live the abundant life which You have prepared for me. Lord, help me to live a life worthy of the calling I've received. I want to live in victory and power! Holy Spirit, please help me today.

I pray this in Jesus' name! Amen.

MY CONFESSION FOR TODAY

I confess I've been given the loin belt of truth. I'm called to stand firm in the truth and everything else in my spiritual life will fall into place. I declare I have been given the breastplate of righteousness. I am in right standing with Christ and I'm covered in His righteousness. I confess I have the shield of faith prepared for me. I'm walking with the Holy Spirit and He is anointing my heart to have faith. I confess I have the helmet of salvation and my mind is clear and protected. Christ died for me and I'm standing in that truth. I confess I have the sword of the Spirit, and watch out — I'm going to use it! I'm tired of living against the wall in my life. I'm standing up straight, putting on my armor, and engaging in the battle of faith.

I declare this by faith in Jesus' name!

MY ACTION STEPS FOR TODAY

1. Take a moment and think about which armor section you need to put on most in your life. Take a moment, consider each piece and ask the Holy Spirit to help you put them on.

2. Has your breastplate of righteousness been pierced through? Do you recognize an area where the devil accuses you that you are not in right standing with God?

3. Take some time and oil up your shield! Put on a favorite worship song and worship Him wholeheartedly or sit in the quietness and begin speaking out praises of thanksgiving for what He is doing in your life. Try not to ask Him for things at this point, but focus on thanking Him for what He has already done and is doing in your life. Thank Him for His protection and provision.

DAY 20
Stay In The Fight

Be sober, be vigilant; because your adversary the devil walks about like a roaring lion, seeking whom he may devour. —1 Peter 5:8

It goes something like this: "You deserve what's happening. If you lived right maybe your life wouldn't be such a mess. You can't ask God to help you because you're the one who got yourself here in the first place. Don't you know a man reaps what he sows?" Have you ever heard this conversation in your mind before? I know I have, too many times to count.

When it comes to spiritual warfare, we can't play the ignorance card. We have to understand we are in a battle. The good news is Jesus already went to Hell and back to guarantee victory, but the devil is still a liar trying to deceive and rob us of our trust and faith in what Jesus did.

Peter writes in his first letter to us to be sober and vigilant. He gives us a vivid picture when he describes the devil as a hungry lion roaming around looking for prey. The word adversary is the Greek work antidikos. This word is used in New Testament times for a lawyer who argues in the court of law.[26] I've come to understand that the devil will never outright lie to us. He usually will pick something we are guilty of. When he accuses us of the sin, we agree and instead of telling him to get lost we make an agreement with the accusations. Then he waits! And at the time when we are most vulnerable he will remind us of our sin and the fact that we agreed we are guilty. At that moment the spiritual wind is knocked out of us and we are left feeling guilty, ashamed and useless. We are embarrassed and our tendency is to run. If

---

26 Renner, Rick. *Sparkling Gems* (Page 652) Published 2003. Print.

we run, we leave the safety of our father and we become a target for the enemy.

I came upon some interesting facts to help make this point as I was doing some research on lions. Most lions will try to draw their prey away from the herd before they attack, and will hunt in the evening or early morning. They heavily rely on the surprise factor which is why they rarely attack during the day due to being easily spotted. I was amazed as I read these facts and could not help but reflect on the spiritual likeness we encounter. Growing up in the church and now having over 20 years of ministry experience, it's not hard to see patterns in people's lives that are very destructive. So many are deceived by the enemy and picked off. It's horrible to watch and my heart hurts every time I hear that someone has walked away from their faith. Most times it happens just as I explained above. Guilt, shame or hurt caused them to leave the flock (body of Christ). The devil whispers lies to entice them to wander off, isolating themselves as they become lone rangers. Then when they least expect it, the enemy surprises them and they are defenseless. I think it's important to note that night is a time to be most on guard. The enemy knows that evening is when we are most alone, tired, or relaxed. Being aware of this can help us never to let our guard down but be vigilant in all hours.

DO ANY OF THESE SOUND FAMILIAR?

- You're in this mess because of your own dumb mistakes!
- You're reaping what you sowed, and there's no way for you to get out of this mess!
- You're paying for your past!
- Your kids are a mess because you failed as a parent!
- You're going to go bankrupt because you spent too much money on worthless things!

- You destroy all your friendships because you are so insecure!

Don't be surprised! Most of us have all heard one, two, or all of these lies. Satan is the god of lies. He is a liar and I hate him! I hate what he does to many of us and I want to see people set free with the knowledge of God; He is the only One who can save us from this bondage.

But enough about the devil, our God is mighty in us! Let's dive in and see what we need to do to stay safe. The word vigilant is used here and comes from the Greek word gregoreo meaning "to be on your guard, to be watchful, or to be attentive". The picture here is the watchful attitude of one who is on the lookout to make certain no enemy or aggressor can successfully gain entry into his life or place of residence.[27]

David told us that the Lord is the One who redeems our lives from destruction (see Psalm 103:4). So, even if we feel defeated, we are not. God is working everything out in our lives for our good because we are called by His purpose. Peter reminds us in 1 Peter 5:9, "Resist him, standing firm in the faith." If you resist the devil, you can run him clear out of your mind and your life. Jesus died on the cross to give us ruling power over the darkness. We have the authority to cast down anything that tries to exalt itself above the knowledge of God (see 1 Corinthians 10:5). It's never going to be about us trying harder or fighting harder. It's about doing all things through Christ who strengthens us (see Philippians 4:13) and sitting back and allowing His Spirit to take charge (Zechariah 4:6). Remember, perfect love casts out fear (see 1 John 4:18), so there is no fear when it comes to defeating the devil. It's just something we have to do until we leave this earth. It will be worth the fight! We have been prepared for war and God is on our side. The entire struggle will at once be removed and we will see the face of Jesus (see Revelation

27 Renner, Rick. Sparkling Gems (Page 652) Published 2003. Print.

21:4). Until then we have to resist the devil, be vigilant, put on our spiritual armor, stay in the Word and spend a ton of time with God. We can do this my friends!

MY PRAYER FOR TODAY

I confess that I am not a weak person! I have the power of God, the name of Jesus Christ and the Word of God at my fingretips. When I choose to step in to my full authority, as a believer, my enemy the devil must take flight. I will no longer allow the devil to torment, shame or harass my mind. Devil, I do not belong to you, I belong to Jesus. I'm coming after you. I'm taking every thought captive and if it doesn't align with the Word of God, it's getting kicked out. I'm on a mission to renew my mind until it comes under the authority of Jesus Christ. I declare this by faith in Jesus' name! Amen.

MY CONFESSION FOR TODAY

I confess I will no longer listen to the lies of the enemy. I will not sit back and allow him to accuse me or provoke me. I do not belong to him and he has no authority over me. I am a sinner saved by grace. I have been given free access to the throne of grace and I'm staying there until further notice. I will not tolerate or negotiate with you, Satan. I'm resisting you and you must flee. Greater is He who is in me than he who is in the world and God is working it all out. I'm called by His name and I'm living in His purpose. I'm not sitting in a helpless position. I am not weak. I'm on my way!

I declare this by faith in Jesus' name! Amen.

MY ACTION STEPS FOR TODAY

1. Take time to identify the most vulnerable areas the enemy lies to you about (example: friendships, marriage, kids, value, etc.) and write them down below.

2. Read Mark 14:21–23 and consider taking communion today by yourself (don't worry if you've never done this before. You don't have to say all the right things; it's always about the heart). Acknowledge your weaknesses, receive God's forgiveness and take time to thank God for the power you have because of Him. Thank Him for the blood that set you free and the body that was given so you no longer have to be alone in the struggle.

FINAL THOUGHTS

As we wrap up and finish this last day of the study, I want to say one thing...WELL DONE! You completed a 20-day journey of engaging with God and regarding your will, your mind, your words and resisting and defeating the enemy. I want to encourage and bless you to continue to walk with power towards a submitted will, a renewed mind, life-giving words, and to stand armed and ready to fight your enemy. I pray that you will truly walk out this "Good Stuff" and be empowered to finish strong!

STUDIES / DEVOTIONALS

I Do Hard Things   Radical Growth   The Good Stuff

TEACHINGS

  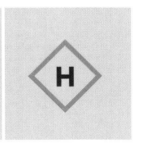

Becoming a Voice   Free Your Mind   Annointed & Qualified

Find these and other great resources at
havilahcunnington.com

STAY CONNECTED

website *havilahcunnington.com*

facebook *Havilah Cunnington*

twitter *@mrshavilah*

instagram *havilahcunnington*

youtube *youtube.com/user/havilahcunnington*

email *info@havilahcunnington.com*

FOR MORE INFORMATION
email info@havilahcunnington.com

join our newsletter

REQUEST HAVILAH TO SPEAK

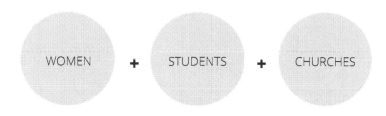

WOMEN **+** STUDENTS **+** CHURCHES

FOR
*Retreats, conferences, one-night gatherings,
church services, leadership events*

THE GOOD STUFF A GUIDEBOOK TO FINISHING STRONG